Finish (almost) Any Quilt

A Simple Guide to Adapting Quilts to *Quilt-As-You-Go*

MW00635303

Loose Fibers Media
PO Box 220245
Anchorage, Alaska 99522-0245
www.loosefibers.com

© 2011 Loose Fibers Media, LLC
All rights reserved
Printed and bound in the United States of America

Third Print Edition

No part of this book may be used or reproduced in any manner without written permission from the publisher, except in the context of reviews or for personal use by the purchaser.

ISBN: 978-1-936826-07-0

The information in this book is presented in good faith; however due to differing conditions, materials, tools, individual skills, creativity, and health conditions, the publisher cannot be responsible for any injuries, losses, and other damages that may result from the use of the information in this book and no results are guaranteed.

Publisher's statement: It is the author's decision to have this book printed locally, on stock paper, not on a high gloss paper. She very much dislikes glossy paper, finding it difficult to read because of reflected lighting. Printing on glossy paper often means printing overseas for cost effectiveness, and she prefers to use local printers.

Editor: Christine Doyle

For Sarah,

who finishes many more quilts than I do

Why Quilt-As-You-Go?   [7]

What this book is about, who it is for, what you should know before jumping in, and what the basic concept is for *finishing-as-you-go*.

1 - Getting Started   [10]

How to plan your quilt project—from unfinished tops to making brand new blocks. What you need to know before beginning, what projects are perfect for *quilt-as-you-go* and what type of projects are not suitable for adaptation.

2 - Building Your Blocks   [32]

Choosing your quilt settings: straight set, on-point setting, wonky setting, a setting that includes built–in borders, plus a section just for T–shirt quilts.

3 - Layering   [58]

Preparing your blocks for quilting. Batting recommendations, smoothing, pinning and more.

4 - Quilting [66]

Simple machine quilting using stitch-in-the-ditch, straight lines, curvy lines, free-motion stippling, and all my best tips for making it easy. Best of all, you are only quilting small individual blocks, not a huge quilt!

5- Joining [88]

How to join your blocks into rows and the rows into a quilt.

6 - Adding Quilted Borders [108]

How to add a quilted border before binding your quilt.

7 - Binding [114]

Easy machine binding and bonus tips for how to make the prettiest corners!

Resources [125]

My deepest thanks to...

Sarah Raffuse, for always listening to my silly ideas and often giving them a try.

Laura McDonell, for sharing her many projects, enthusiasm and cherished support.

Mary Couch, for sharing her *Turning Twenty* quilt on page 12.

Debbie Caffrey, for allowing the use of her *Quilter's Threads* pattern on page 16.

Ruth Blanchet, for allowing the use of her *Bargello Blues* quilt photo on page 17.

Pamela Harris, for sharing her story and her gorgeous art quilt on page 18. Her quilt was an inspiration to me while writing this book.

Elizabeth Haines, for her inspiration while writing this book, and for sharing her *Ohio Star Quilt* and its story on page 19.

Sue Pelland, for her *Leaves Galore* rulers that I used on the quilt on page 109.

Arteria McCummings for her thoughtful suggestions and advice.

Introduction

This is not a traditional quilt book! In fact, I am asking you to re-think how quilts are put together from beginning to end.

What that means is: If you skim the book, you might not understand why things are in the order that they are. If you read all the way through, or make a project with me, it all falls into place.

There are no quilt patterns in this book. Rather, there are design options to take what you have now, or quilts that you want to make, and *finish* them using my quilt-as-you-go method.

The quilt-as-you-go method allows you to take projects you've started or patterns you want to make and adapt them into blocks that you can easily quilt and then join together. The process is a simple one that allows for many variations that will make your quilt uniquely your own.

Here's the process you'll follow to finish your quilts:

- Build up your blocks with borders
- Quilt the blocks using easy machine stitching
- Trim the blocks to a uniform size
- Join your blocks into rows
- Join your rows into a quilt
- Bind your quilt all by machine
- Start to finish your next quilt!

Who This Book Is For

If you are a brand–new quilt maker who has been intimidated by the idea of trying to quilt a huge quilt, I hope you'll read this book with inspiration, and then find a block that you like and make your own quilt, your way, and finish it with me. You will be surprised at how quickly you will have a finished quilt on your bed!

If you are an intermediate quilt maker who is tired of struggling to machine quilt your own quilts on your home sewing machine, I hope you'll find inspiration in my machine quilting techniques. You'll see how easy it is to put together a *finished* quilt using the methods in this book.

If you are an experienced quilt maker, let's turn, "I *should* finish these quilts" into, "I can finish my quilts *this way!* I like this look, and I'm sure I can do it!"

If you've vowed, "No new projects until I finish *something,*" let's finish your quilts together in a whole new way, quickly and easily.

You loved your quilt projects when you started them; now let's pull them out, and fall in love with them again, and finish them in lots of new ways! If you are a perfectionist, this may

not be the book for you. I break a lot of traditional rules, and you may not like it.

If you want to make award–winning, blue–ribbon quilts, this is definitely not the book for you, because I don't follow traditional rules. If you want to *finish* lots of quilts *easily*, this book is **just for you**!

If you:

- love playing with blocks
- want to finish your quilts yourself
- like change and adaptations
- are open to new ideas

then this is the book for you!

This book will give you confidence, step-by-step tips, fabric calculations, ideas and inspiration, and permission to finish an already-started project *any way that you want*.

1. Getting Started

If you have unfinished projects, pull them out now, and let's see what it takes to finish them.

If you want to start a new project, grab your block book or pattern and follow along!

I'll show you which blocks and patterns work and which ones don't suit this quick process, and you'll learn how to adapt what you have to make it *finish*-as-you-go.

I change around the order of the steps from traditional quilt making, so read through first, before cutting your fabric, and get ready to re-think how you make and *finish* your quilts!

Getting Started

I know you want to jump right in to finishing your quilts. But before we do, here are a few terms and techniques that I refer to throughout the book. Take a few minutes to review this section so you're ready to get started.

Sewing Machine Parts

The **feed dogs** are the teeth under the presser foot. On some sewing machines, there's a lever or control for dropping the feed dogs, and that's very useful for free–motion quilting. The **throat** of a sewing machine is the open area between the needle and the motor.

The **presser foot** attaches to the shaft or shank of the sewing machine. Presser feet are interchangeable, and the best one for each project or type of sewing is suggested in several places in this book. A *walking foot* or *even feed foot* is a specialized presser foot. If you are not familiar with your sewing machine's presser feet, review your owner's manual.

The **pressure setting** is a control for how much downward pressure the sewing machine puts on the presser foot. Often too much pressure results in wrinkles and puckers in the quilt, especially while machine quilting straight lines.

I use and recommend a 90/14 sharp quilting **needle** for piecing and machine quilting, and I recommend cleaning and oiling your machine (according to the manufacturer's instructions) before starting a new project.

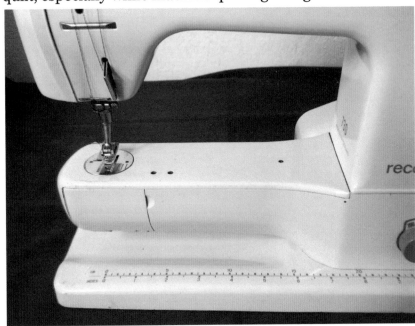

I have many videos on YouTube about sewing and quilting. For some visual tips, please visit http://www.youtube.com/crazyshortcutquilts

Fabric

I use, and recommend using, 100% cotton fabric for quilting. Most cotton fabric comes on a bolt, folded in half, and is 40"-44" wide when unfolded. The printed, or stiff, edges run opposite the fold and are called the **selvages**. Selvages should be cut off before using your fabric.

The **lengthwise grain** runs in the same direction as the fold and the selvage. It is the strongest and most stable grain. It's very difficult to stretch a fabric on the lengthwise grain. For this reason, I cut everything I can along the lengthwise grain. The **crosswise grain** runs on the cut edge of the fabric, and it has a nice stretch to it. I try not to cut my joining strips along this grain.

What does this mean in terms of buying fabric? If you needed a piece of fabric that is 2" wide and 12" long, it might seem to make sense to buy 2" off the fabric on the bolt, on the crosswise grain, then cut 12" from that 42" strip.

However, if you want that strip of fabric to be un-stretchable, then you would cut it from the lengthwise grain, buying 12" of fabric and then cutting a 2" strip off that fabric, after trimming off the selvage.

If the selvage is not on your fabric, and you are unsure of the grain lines on it, stretch it gently to find the grain. There will be a slight stretch on the crosswise grain and no stretch on the lengthwise grain.

Selecting fabric colors is a subject of many books, and it's not something that I am good at. If, like me, you struggle with this, bring a friend shopping with you and don't hesitate to ask anyone in the store for help—employees and other shoppers alike. I've struck up some wonderful conversations while fabric shopping!

As a general rule, I don't prewash my fabrics, but my daughter Sarah always prewashes hers. It's entirely up to you. If you do pre-wash, snip all four corners of your yardage before putting it in the wash to avoid lots of tangled threads.

Pressing

Pressing is a "lift up, press down" movement that is not the same as ironing. **When pressing quilt blocks, there should be no movement of the iron**. Just press the iron straight down and lift it up, move to another spot, press straight down and lift up. Any movement of the iron can distort the piecing in quilt blocks.

On most projects, I starch the fabric while pressing, using a spray bottle and a mix of commercial liquid starch to 3 parts filtered water. You can save money and control the strength of your starch by mixing your own solution and using a spray bottle. Concentrated starch is available at grocery stores and the larger chain stores.

I starch heavily before using any fabrics. I almost soak my fabric in starch, knowing that the quilt will soon be washed. In fact, some quilters prefer to prepare

a starch solution in a bucket, dunk their fabrics, then let the fabric hang over the bathtub to dry overnight before pressing.

There are many recipes for starch, including some that use essential oils for a lovely fragrance if you prefer to make your own.

I will often use a pressing cloth (usually just a piece of muslin) to keep the starch from building up on my iron.

Fiber artist Mary Couch adapted the popular pattern <u>Turning Twenty</u> into quilt-as-you-go. Notice her added cat appliques?

A quilt-as-you-go quilt requires blocks that you can join together with joining strips. Beyond that, though, there are many factors to consider with each project. Look at all of the projects in this book, making notes on variations that you like and how you can use what you like best in your quilts, because it's all interchangeable. Any size border can be added to your blocks, and you can choose any block setting.

As you read through the process, make note of your desired finished quilt size and the size of the blocks that you have. You can adjust your project to obtain the desired finished size quilt by changing the size of the block borders or by adding a quilted border.

So much goes into planning a quilt, and even more goes into re-working a pattern. I've done my best to give you solid examples in this book, from unfinished projects to brand–new projects. Your challenge is to decide which design layouts you like best and how you'd like your finished quilts to look.

Most of all, have fun imagining all the ways you can finish your quilts today!

Starting with UFOs

Nicknamed "Unfinished Objects", many quilters have projects that have been set aside for one reason or another. Maybe the technique is one that became boring or too much work, or you may have changed your mind about how much you liked the fabrics. Or perhaps some other, more fascinating, quilt called out to you, and you set the quilt project aside.

Unless you bought more fabric than your pattern called for, you may not have enough fabric to convert your existing quilt to finish-as-you-go. This means that, if you were bored with the fabrics, now's your chance change that around. You can change the entire look of the quilt with some new fabrics.

Take a look at your pattern and your blocks. Some may not adapt well to the techniques in this book, but hope you'll keep an open mind and consider all the options given. Remember your goal is to have a finished quilt.

By changing your project to fit the techniques in this book, you'll be excited to work on it again. Best of all, you're halfway there if you've already made the blocks!

Unfinished Block Quilts

Are your blocks square? Do they "stand alone", meaning can they be surrounded by fabric (wide or narrow — it's your choice) and still maintain the look you want?

Appliqué and embroidery blocks are the easiest to adapt to finishing as you go because they often have a much greater seam allowance than ¼", which means you don't have to add any block borders. You can go right to quilting and joining your blocks, especially if you don't want to make the quilt larger that what the original pattern calls for.

Blocks that are pieced and applique blocks that have only a ¼" seam allowance on the edges of the blocks need to have additional fabric attached to each block so that the joining strips, which have a seam allowance wider than ½", can be sewn on without sewing over the details of the blocks.

Unfinished Quilt Tops

I don't think that any of us likes to un-sew a project. However, it usually takes only a little bit of seam ripping to take a quilt top apart into easily manageable pieces.

Easier yet, if there's enough fabric between blocks, you can cut the top through the sashing and add another border to each block.

If your quilt has a wide outer border, deconstructing the quilt may change the size of the quilt, so you may need additional fabric, or a whole new border, to bring it back to the finished size you desire.

Learn more about built–in borders on page 47.

On this little top, I plan to cut through the inner sashing, trim off the outer border, and add a "built–in" outer border.

Starting from a Quilt Pattern

The easiest way to convert any quilt project is to start with the pattern first, before ever buying or cutting your fabric. Once you've converted a pattern to quilt-as-you-go you will be able to look at every pattern you see from now on and easily tell if it is convertible.

The easiest pattern to convert is one made up of blocks with wide borders around them, or with wide sashing between the blocks. You can buy extra border fabric to use to make the block borders (or sashing) wider than the pattern calls for and to use as the top joining strips.

Analyze the Pattern

If you see obvious grid lines in your pattern, it can be adapted to the methods in this book. If there are no grid lines, but there are spaces between the blocks, you can easily convert the pattern by making the background block fabric slightly larger than the pattern calls for and by buying extra fabric for the joining strips.

Even if the grid lines are not perfect squares, if there are straight lines in the pattern, it can be subdivided into blocks (square or rectangle). Those blocks can be quilted and joined into rows along the straight lines of the pattern, and then the rows can be joined into a finished quilt.

You may even want to disregard the pattern altogether once the blocks are pieced.

Soon when you buy a new pattern, you'll start looking at only the blocks and not the entire pattern. You may find yourself using a book on just how to make blocks for your quilts along with this book on how to build up and finish your blocks into a quilt.

I've always loved this spools pattern by Debbie Caffrey. Because the spool blocks are built individually, it would be easy to add straight block borders to each one.

The secondary pattern of the pinwheel, made from the wooden ends of the spools, would be lost by adding borders to each block. But that small design element could be replaced with a new design element if the block were made "wonky" or by using scraps that match the "thread" colors on each spool for block borders.

When considering a new pattern, take a look at the overall design and decide if you can live with the change of adding a fabric border to the blocks that make up the quilt.

This design element will be eliminated.

In the case of this pattern, I'd happily forego the pinwheels created by the spool ends in favor of a wonky setting. This adapted pattern would have a real tumbled look, similar to what I see whenever I look in my thread drawers!

Not All Quilt Designs Are Adaptable

Some quilt designs are not ascetically adaptable to the techniques in this book. Tessellations, Bargellos, Courthouse Steps, Wedding Ring (interlocking rings), Trip Around The World, Lonestar and Ocean Waves (triangles) would lose an important element of their gorgeous overall design if changed.

I'm not saying they can't be finished this way, but the overall quilt design would be changed significantly, and you might not be happy with the finished quilt.

Any pattern that has a block design that connects with the block next to it for the overall quilt design should be looked at closely before adapting.

Ruth Blanchet's "Bargello Blues" quilt would lose its lovely flowing lines if converted to this method.

Customizing your Blocks and Borders

Whether you start with UFOs or a pattern, there are lots of ways to customize the blocks and borders for a unique quilt. Here are just three examples.

Combine Small Blocks

If you are a fan of the many historical quilts being reintroduced today in 4½″ to 6″ block size, consider grouping four or more blocks into one larger block and adding a border to it. For instance, if you have a quilt made up of 6″ blocks, you could group four together, using an inner sashing and outer border, to make a 16″ block. Or group nine together to make an 18″ block, then add borders to that block.

Turn Your Blocks Into Art

Pamela Harris was inspired to spice up some blocks from an exchange she participated in with a Fairbanks, Alaska, quilt guild. She slashed the blocks and sewed in bright, colorful strips of fabric. She made both the blocks and the bright strips "pop" with her dual color borders and sashing strips.

Photo courtesy of Pamela Harris.

I felt tremendous inspiration when I first saw Pam's quilt. She has combined traditional and modern styles with stunning effect.

As someone who gathers blocks and projects from many sources, I cheer her process of taking many different blocks and making them into a quilt that is unique, artistic and special to her.

Notice the simple curved quilting on her quilt borders? We'll be trying that out in the Quilting chapter.

Although Pam's quilt is not done with a quilt-as-you-go technique, do you see how it could have been, with the narrow strips between the blocks as the joining strips?

By adding cream borders to these finished blocks and using blue joining strips, Elizabeth Haines was able to finish this quilt using quilt-as-you-go.

Rethink Your Borders

Elizabeth Haines customized an Ohio Star quilt project to obtain the look that she and her daughter and son-in-law wanted for a quilt that was going in the young family's new home.

She writes, "My daughter and her husband picked out the fabrics (a Moda stack of fat quarters), and they cut and stitched the first 24 blocks...I just talked them into letting me finish, as they are in that busy stage of life with a two-year-old!"

Elizabeth added the cream border to the blocks and then widened (to 2½″) the top joining strips (blue) and the back joining strips (to 1⅝″) to create an additional border look with the joining strips. She increased our "fat ¼″ seam" to ⅜″ and she also created a pieced border.

I absolutely love that Elizabeth created such a gorgeous quilt, adapting the quilt-as-you-go methods to give her the results she was looking for!

Determining Your Style

Let's look at some quilts and get an idea of how adapting them might change the way those patterns look. Don't worry about the machine quilting yet; let's just start with the overall look of the quilt and what appeals to you.

Take a Look at Finished Quilts

Take a look not only at the quilts in this book, but at finished quilts in general. Look at your collection of books, patterns, and magazines and see what style of quilt you like best. Are they traditional, modern, scrappy? Do you love piecing or appliqué? Are the settings that you like large, with wide sashing between the blocks? Or do you like a tightly packed look, busy with blocks and no sashing or inner borders at all?

Flip back and forth between the quilts shown in this book and the quilts you like and look for similarities that will let you adapt the quilts you like to a style that will help you finish those quilts easily.

Visible or Hidden Joining Strips?

The biggest decision you will need to make for each quilt that you adjust is the width of any block borders you add and the choice of fabrics you want to use for your joining strips.

You may want the joining strips to be seen as a part of the quilt pattern or you might want them hidden, blending in with the block borders, to look like one large sashing.

Sarah's quilt (opposite) has very a obvious grid with its contrasting fabric joining strips. The blue scrappy stars quilt on page 22 has joining strips from the same material as the block border, which helps them blend in. The pink stars quilt on page 49 has almost invisible joining strips.

Choose a Back

The back of the quilt uses its own set of joining strips, and it's your choice to make them blend or stand out, as well. The back of your quilt can be every bit

Bright Idea by Sarah Raffuse from the book **Crazy Shortcut Quilts**. In this quilt, the joining strips are obvious and become part of the quilt's design.

Here the joining strips on the front blend in with the block borders. But on the back, the joining strips complement the fabric, rather than match it.

as interesting as the front, and it's a great place to feature some big–print fabric that you love.

You might choose to use fabrics that complement the top of your quilt on the back or leftover fabrics from the top of your quilt. Or if you want your quilt to have the same look on both sides, you can checkerboard it by reversing every other block so that the top and back look exactly the same.

Some of my very favorite fabrics to use as backings are large prints that I really don't want to cut up. By using those fabrics as backing, I get a whole quilt made from them whenever I flip over my quilt.

I'd been hoarding these teacups and plates fabrics (opposite) for a long time, just waiting to make a quilt with blocks large enough to be able to use them. These 19" scrappy blocks worked out perfectly. I love both sides of my quilt!

On this quilt I am getting ready to put on the binding. Can you see the joining strips between the blocks, covered by the curvy stitching? The joining strips blend in quite well with this small-print fabric.

26

You can barely see the joining strip grid on the back of this quilt; it looks like all one fabric because of the very small print used. The joining strips are also completely hidden on the top of this red-and-white quilt.

Making a Fabric and Batting Plan

The measurements given here are generous because all binding, joining strips, and block borders are cut on the lengthwise grain, which requires more yardage than cutting on the crosswise grain.

The reason for this is explained fully in the Joining chapter. But it's basically the only thing that I strongly emphasize in this entire book and it's a practice that firmly adhere to. I've learned the hard way, and I ask you to trust me on this.

In addition to the fabric you'll need for block borders, you will need fabric for joining strips and probably more batting and backing than called for in your original pattern.

The fabric needed for block borders is <u>not</u> included in the fabric suggestions on the next two pages. See pages 42 and 43 of the Building Your Blocks chapter for those recommendations.

Because quilt sizes vary, it's not possible to know exactly how much fabric you'll need. Therefore I'm calling these *suggestions*, not requirements, and I've separated them by the finished size of quilt that they help make.

Although I can't be exact, I can be very close, without underestimating, and my philosophy is, "You can never buy too much fabric." In most cases, these are generous fabric suggestions for the joining strips, batting, and backing.

The joining strip fabric suggestions are based on a fairly large block—12″ to 15″. If your blocks are smaller than this, you'll need more fabric because the more blocks you have, the more joining strips you need, and therefore, the more fabric you need. So for smaller blocks, add at least ½ yard to the smaller-sized quilts. Add up to 1 yard for the medium-sized quilts, and add 2 yards for the largest quilts.

None of the fabric suggestions given take into account any outside quilted borders or block borders. If you intend to add a quilted border, you will need to increase the amount of fabric accordingly. For specifics, see the Adding Quilted Borders chapter. If back joining strip fabric is listed separately and you want them to be the same fabric as your backing, add the two measurements together.

Here's my very best fabric tip: ***always buy more fabric and batting than you think you're going to need.***

A small quilt (up to 36″ x 45″) of twenty 9″ blocks

1 yard fabric for all the joining strips (top and back) & binding **or**

1 yard fabric for top joining strips & binding **and**
½ yard fabric for the back joining strips

1⅓ yards backing fabric
1¼ yard batting at 45″ wide

A small quilt (up to 48″ x 48″) of nine 16″ blocks

1 yard fabric for all the joining strips (top and back) & binding **or**

1 yard fabric for top joining strips & binding **and**
½ yard fabric for the back joining strips

2½ yards backing fabric
2⅔ yards batting at 45″ wide or 1¼ yards at 90″ wide

A small to medium quilt (up to 48″x 64″) of twelve 16″ blocks

2 yards fabric for all the joining strips (top and back) & binding **or**

1 yard fabric for the only the top joining strips and the binding **and**
½ yard fabric for the back joining strips

3 yards backing fabric
3 yards batting at 45″ wide or 1½ yards at 90″ wide

A medium quilt (up to 60″ x 60″) of sixteen 15″ blocks

2 yards fabric for all the joining strips (top and back) & binding **or**

1¾ yards fabric for top joining strips & binding **and**
½ yard fabric for the back joining strips

4 yards backing fabric
4 yards batting at 45″ wide or 2 yards batting at 90″ wide

All calculations are based upon 40″ width of usable fabric.

A medium quilt (up to 60″ x 72″) of thirty 12″ blocks*

2½ yards fabric for all the joining strips (top and back) & binding **or**

1¾ yards fabric for the top joining strips & binding **and**
1 yard fabric for the back joining strips

3⅓ yards backing and 1¾ yards batting at 90″ wide

> * I've included this measurement especially for quilters who love small blocks like the very popular 6″ Civil War blocks. See **Combine Small Blocks** on page 21.

A medium to large quilt (up to 60″ x 75″) of twenty 15″ blocks

2½ yards fabric for all the joining strips (top and back) & binding **or**

1¾ yards fabric for top joining strips & binding **and**
½ yard fabric for the back joining strips

5 yards backing fabric and 2 yards batting at 90″ wide

A large quilt (up to 80″ x 96″) of thirty 16″ blocks

2½ yards fabric for only the joining strips (top and back) **and**
1⅓ yards fabric for the binding **or**

1½ yards fabric for top joining strips **and**
1 yard fabric for the back joining strips **and**
1⅓ yards fabric for the binding

7 ½ yards backing fabric and 3 yards batting at 90″ wide

A larger quilt (up to 112″ x 128″) of fifty six 16″ blocks

5 yards fabric for only the joining strips (top and back) **and**
3 yards fabric for the binding **or**

3 yards fabric for top joining strips **and**
2 fabric yards for the back joining strips

14 yards backing fabric and 6 yards batting at 90″ wide

Estimating for Larger Blocks

If your quilt blocks are larger than those on the chart, calculate how wide your finished quilt will be, after adding any borders to the blocks, and buy slightly more than that measurement of fabric for binding and top joining strips.

For instance, if my finished quilt will measure 55″ wide, I would buy 60″ (1⅔ yards) of fabric for the top joining strips and binding. This is a general estimate and should give you plenty of fabric with some left over.

This saves from having to piece (connect or join) a whole lot of short strips when making the binding and row joining strips. There will be fabric left over, which I personally prefer over being caught short. I am a scrap lover and saver, so all the extra fabric goes right into my scrap fabrics bin for another quilt.

I suggest buying slightly more fabric than the width of your quilt because often the fabric will need to be trimmed on both ends to give it a clean edge.

There's no point in buying the exact length you need, to the inch. Too often you'll have to trim it and end up 2″ short, then you'll need to piece little bits in just to have the right length of row joining strips.

Planning Your Fabric Cutting

You'll find several times in this book that I talk about cutting order, or the sequence that I use for cutting fabrics, to allow for flexibility in the quilt design as it is being made. You might start your quilt planning on having 10″ blocks and then change your mind and add fabric to make them larger. If you've already cut your block joining strips to 10″, that change of plans will make those strips useless for your quilt.

In general, when using all the same fabrics for the top of a medium to large size quilt, I cut my block border strip fabric as one large piece (and cut the strips from that piece) from the width of fabric, then I cut the binding strips and row joining strips from the *length* of fabric. I don't trim the binding or row joining strips to their exact length until they are actually needed, I just cut the strips off the yardage and set them aside. The fabric that is left is used for the block joining strips and is cut to size *after* my blocks are quilted and trimmed.

Starting with Pieced Blocks

If your unfinished projects are stacks of pieced blocks, hurray! You are almost ready to quilt them and join the quilted blocks into a finished quilt.

The first step is deciding what type of block borders to add. Your borders can be straight fabric strips, wonky strips, triangles (for an on-point setting), or asymmetrical strips for a built-in outer border on your quilt.

I don't recommend jumping straight from pieced blocks to quilting because the joining strips that are used to connect the blocks use more than a ¼″ seam allowance. If your blocks have only an excess of ¼″ fabric on any or all sides, the block design will be covered by the joining strips. So the block borders serve to protect your points and piecing.

Starting with Embroidery and Appliqué Blocks

Many appliquéd, embroidered and redwork blocks will have lots of room around the edges. You can go right to the quilting stage, bypassing adding block borders completely, if you want.

You might choose, however, to add some borders: straight, wonky, triangles for an on-point setting or even asymmetrical strips for a built-in outer border on your quilt. You can use block borders to make your quilt bigger or to emphasize a certain color by bringing in a new fabric.

Starting with T–shirts

The techniques in this book are perfect for making T–shirt quilts! If you've never sewn knitted fabric, you might not know how different it is from sewing cotton fabric. It's incredibly helpful to stabilize the fabric, and personal preference is going to play a large part here.

Many people stabilize knits with an iron-on stabilizer; however I prefer to stabilize knit T–shirts with liquid starch (which is not the same as spray starch). I find that both 100% starch, or a 50-50 solution of starch and water, works well. When the quilt is finished, I immediately wash it to remove all the starch, and I love the soft feeling of the knit once the starch is washed out. I prefer this method because there's no left–over stiffness like there can be with permanent stabilizers.

I highly recommend pre-shrinking all of the fabrics that are to be used in your T–shirt quilt: all block border fabrics, joining fabrics, binding and cotton batting, if your batting allows (not all battings hold up to pre-washing).

Cut the area to be used from the shirt and be very generous. Use your favorite stabilizer and completely stabilize an area larger than what you plan on using.

If you are using my liquid starch method, fill a bowl or small bucket with starch. Dunk the dry fabric in, and gently squeeze out most of the excess liquid. Or you can spread the fabric out and just pour the starch on it, spreading it around with your fingers. Either way, the fabric will be soaked and you'll need to dry

The T–shirt fabric is stiff as a board after soaking in starch and air drying flat.

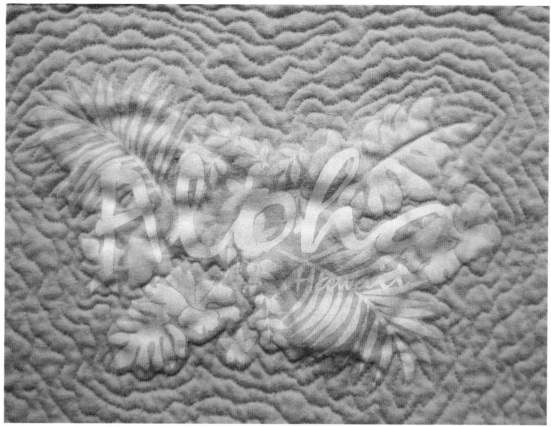

In this example, nothing was pre–washed and the T–shirt fabric "poofed" up when washed.

the pieces flat. To do otherwise would distort the fabric or let the starch settle unevenly. The goal is to get an even saturation of starch throughout the knitted fabric, and to dry it so that it is flat and as stiff as a board in order to stabilize it for quilting. This can be time consuming if you have many tees, but I really feel it's worth it for that soft feeling that I want for my quilts. If you don't pre-wash the other fabrics in the quilt, they will shrink but the tee shirt won't. If your quilt is decorative and not going to be washed, or you don't mind the poofiness that may happen when washed, skip the pre-washing.

Add block borders to the logo or design of the shirts until all blocks are of uniform size. You can even add in some traditional quilt blocks in with your T–shirts for a very unique and eclectic quilt.

I recommend quilting T–shirt blocks with a good density of quilting, leaving no more than a 2″ gap between quilting lines. Knits will stretch and may "bag" away from the batting and backing without enough quilting. If you find that happening to a finished quilt, just add a little bit more quilting.

Starting with Rows

If you already have your quilt blocks put together into rows, you can actually quilt it and then jump right into joining rows, **if you have enough fabric on the rows to allow for the quilting and some trimming.** Remember that the joining strips take more than ¼″ of fabric. If your row has only ¼″ seam allowance, you'll want to add fabric strips to the rows before layering and quilting.

Starting with Quilt Tops

If you have an unfinished quilt top, and it uses sashing or inner borders, it's going to be your choice if you want to cut it or take the stitching out. I know that it sounds cumbersome and time consuming, but I prefer to take the stitching out, especially if the inner sashing is narrow. I like to have a lot of fabric around my blocks, and I want as few seams as possible to quilt over. So I put on some relaxing music and set up a comfortable, well lit area, and I take the quilt apart.

If your quilt top does not have obvious blocks that can be separated from the others without losing the design element, you have two choices. You can forego the design element, in favor of finishing the quilt, or you can quilt it the traditional way, as a whole quilt. It's a difficult decision, so I urge you to think about how the finished quilt will look. Will you still like it if the design elements are changed?

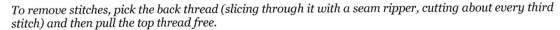

To remove stitches, pick the back thread (slicing through it with a seam ripper, cutting about every third stitch) and then pull the top thread free.

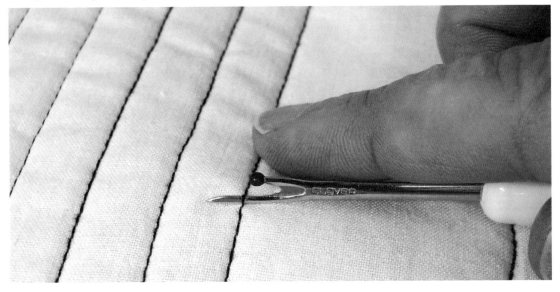

Preparing Your Blocks and Border Fabric

Because all of my quilts are to be used, washed, and loved, I believe in starch, heavy starch. **By starching all of your fabrics**, including blocks you may have already made, **you'll be making the process of quilting**—the actual machine quilting of the three layers—**much easier**.

Stiff fabrics are easy to move and easy to sew through. I can't emphasize this enough. If you are pulling out blocks you made in the past, freshen them up with pressing and lots of starch. Press and heavily starch all of the additional fabrics you are going to use to make your quilt to make them easier to quilt.

If your blocks have ragged edges, don't worry. You can trim them straight if you want, or you can use the edge of your border strip as a straight line to follow and just sew a straight seam.

If your blocks vary in sizes a great deal, you can add an inner border to the smaller blocks, building them up, or you can make all of the border strips large and trim all the blocks to one size after they have been quilted.

Before deciding on what fabric to use, or how wide to make the block borders, audition the fabric by putting your blocks right on it. You could use a design wall, bed or floor to do this. Once the blocks are laying on the fabric, move them around to see how wide you want the fabric between the blocks.

The fabrics that you choose as block borders won't stay whole, however. The joining strips divide the blocks right down the middle. If you want your block borders and joining strips to blend together, choose a small print or solid color for both.

Balance,

like beauty,

is in the eye

of the beholder.

I love the background fabric shown here, and I had hoped that it would work well as block borders for the applique blocks. But the little quilters on the fabric would end up being cut too small to be recognizable and that's not what I want to have happen to this fabric.

The "quilters" fabric might make a better outer border to show off the fabric, with the gold fabric as the block borders.

The gorgeous embroidery blocks are turned every which way. Here I am testing the color of the fabric against the color of the threads in the blocks.

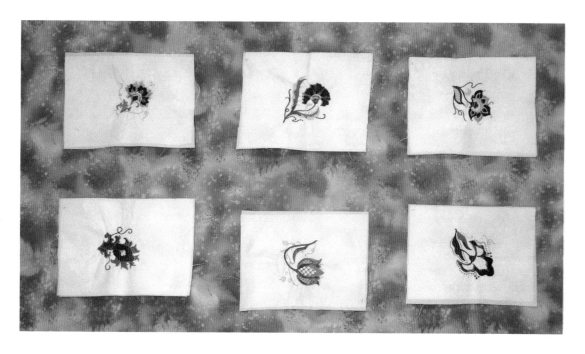

Which one would you choose? Or would you use both colors, adding two borders to each block? If so, which color border would you prefer on the inside and which on the outside?

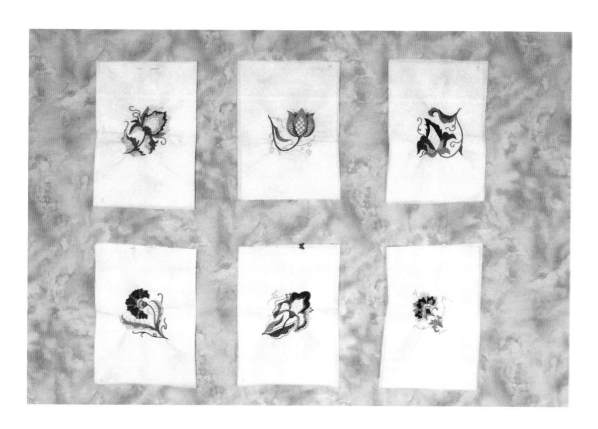

Adding Borders to Your Blocks

For simplicity's sake, I am suggesting only four options for adding single borders to your blocks. Of course you could come up with all kinds of fun ways to incorporate additional designs or multiple borders, and I hope that you will explore any creative ideas sparked by the basic instructions. Remember, it's **your** quilt, you do whatever makes **you** happiest with it!

Before you add any block borders, you'll need to calculate fabric. I recommend you review the Planning chapter on fabric suggestions for the joining strips, batting, and backing.

Review the chart opposite for block border fabric estimates. Note that I recommend cutting your block border fabric 1″ wider than the desired finish size. This allows for shrinkage due to quilting and trimming.

If you want to calculate your own border sizes, I have a few tips. As a general rule allow for ¼″ to be taken up by the seam allowance used to sew the border to the block and allow for up to ¾″ to be taken up by quilting and trimming the block. So for the border size that you want, add at least 1″ extra.

If you plan on quilting your blocks heavily, with very dense quilting, I suggest adding an extra ½″ to 1″, so the calculation on the opposite page would be Desired Border Width + 1 ½″ to 2″.

For example, if you have 8½″ blocks, and your intention is to have a 2½″ visible border between blocks and rows, I recommend adding 2¼″ wide border strips to each block. ¼″ of this will be used in the seam allowance, leaving 2″. Allow for ¾″ of this to be taken up with quilting and trimming, leaving 1¼″ extra all around your block. When that 1¼″ is matched up to the next block's 1¼″ border you'll have a 2½″ sashing between blocks. If you plan on doing very dense quilting on your blocks, double the quilting and trimming allowance to 1½″ and add ¼″ for seam allowance.

If you decide to add multiple block borders, adjust the measurements of each accordingly. If you go over 3″ in your borders, change the allowance for quilting and trimming from ¾″ to 1″ or more for regular quilting and to 2″ or more for dense quilting.

Always add the block border pieces to opposite sides of the blocks. You can chain piece your border strips while sewing them on, just like with normal block piecing.

Below are very general fabric estimations. Use the recommendations for the listing that most closely matches your project in terms of block size and desired border width or setting. Double the Fabric Needed numbers if you have double the number of blocks.

Straight Borders & Building in An Outer Border

Desired Block Size	Number of blocks	Border Width	Cut Width	Fabric Needed
5" Block	20	1"	2"	¾ yard
10" Block	12	1"	2"	1¼ yards
10" Block	12	2'	3"	1½ yards
15" Block	12	1"	2"	1⅔ yards
15" Block	12	2"	3"	2 yards
15" Block	12	3"	4"	2½ yards

Wonky Borders

Desired Block Size	Number of blocks	Cut Width	Fabric Needed
5" Block	20	4"	1 yard
10" Block	12	4"	1⅓ yards
15" Block	12	4"	1⅔ yards

On Point Setting

Desired Block Size	Number of blocks	Cut Squares	Fabric Needed
5" Block	20	5"	½ yard
10" Block	12	10"	1 yard
15" Block	12	15"	3½ yards

I've added 2½" block borders to this scrappy block. The dark blue is the design wall behind the block.

Adding Straight Block Borders

Adding straight borders is the easiest and fastest way to finish a block quilt.

Here's the basic process for adding block borders. For any size quilt block, the process is the same.

1. Measure your blocks and cut two border strips for every block, using your desired width and the exact length of the block. For example 2″ x 15″ for a 15″ block.
2. Sew the border strips to opposite sides of each block.
3. Press the seams toward the border strips.
4. Measure the length of the remaining sides of the block and cut 2 border strips for each block using your new block length measurement and desired width.
5. Sew the border strips to the remaining two opposite sides of each block.
6. Press the seams toward the border strips.
7. Layer the blocks for quilting, but **do not trim or square the blocks yet**.

Once you have added your borders, you may want to put your blocks on your design wall or lay them out on a bed to see if the final look makes you happy. You can add more borders, trim down the borders you added, or twist them up to make them wonky. Now's the time to make any changes, before layering and quilting.

For the quilt below, I started with 15½″ pieced blocks, but they varied in size by ½″ or so. To solve this problem, I added 2½″ block borders to the blocks. After quilting, I trimmed the blocks to 19″, which left 2¼″ borders on all sides. Now all the blocks were the same size even though some of the pieced portions were still a bit smaller.

Take a look at the finished quilt on page 46 and notice that by using a single width border on all sides of the blocks and a matching joining fabric, the quilt has a wider sashing between blocks than on the outer border. If you prefer a more even look to your inner and outer borders, a method for achieving that is described in the next section.

For fabric requirements for adding this type of border to your blocks see page 43.

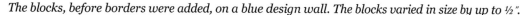

The blocks, before borders were added, on a blue design wall. The blocks varied in size by up to ½″.

This block will be placed in the upper left corner of the finished quilt, so the left and top block borders are wider.

Building in an Outer Border

This type of block border creates a built-in outer border for your quilt, with wider block border strips on some blocks, based on where that block is in the quilt layout. This is a little more complicated to plan out but creates a gorgeous quilt.

Review the Layout process on page 91 and choose your desired layout before beginning this quilt, because once the border strips are added to the blocks, the option for changing their placement becomes very limited. I find it helpful to write the block's position on its layout tag. Each block tag has the row, block number and says either *corner, edge* or *inner square*. This is my way of making sure that I put the correct border strip on the appropriate edge of each block.

Read through the section on Adding Straight Block Borders because the process of sewing the border strips is exactly the same. When calculating the fabric for Straight Borders (page 43) be sure to use the width you want for your **outside** border as the Desired Border Width. To attain this look, your top joining fabric must be the same as your block border fabric, and it should blend well with itself—such as a solid fabric or small print fabric would do.

From left to right, these blocks will be placed in the bottom row, the center, and the top row of the quilt.

The measurements that I used for the border strips on my 10½″ blocks above are 2″ on the inner portions of the blocks and 3½″ on the outer portions—the edges of the quilt.

To plan this quilt, place your blocks on your border fabric and move the blocks around to see what size borders you want. Then measure the spaces between the blocks and the outer edge of the fabric.

For my quilt, here, the four corner blocks have wider border strips on two sides. All of the other outer blocks, along the edge of the quilt, have a wider strip on one side only. The inner blocks all have narrow width border strips.

Decide what width you'd like for your block borders, both for the *inner border* and the *outer quilt border*. Remember, they don't have to be the same size. Your outer border could be a different width than the rest of the inner borders, wider or narrower.

For your outer block border pieces, add 1″ to the desired finished width (to allow for seam allowance and shrinkage during quilting and trimming) and cut your border pieces to that width, matching the length of the block.

The block on the left has the narrowest borders, it is an inner block.

The center block is a corner, with two wide block borders.

The right block is an outer border block, with just one wider border.

For your inner borders divide your desired finished width between the blocks by 2 and then add 1″ to that measurement. For instance, if you want a finished width between your blocks of 3″, divide that by 2 (which gives you 1½″) and then add 1″, so you would cut your inner border strips 2½″ wide by the length of the block.

Notice the varying width borders on these blocks? Look at the bottom photo, upper left corner of the finished quilt to find these blocks.

As you sew, you will still add your block border strips in pairs, on opposite sides of each block. Don't cut all of your border strips at one time. Cut your first set of block borders and sew them on, then measure for the second set of borders, after you recalculate the **length** of the second set of border strips.

Don't trim your blocks after adding the borders, just press and layer for quilting.

When trimming your squares **after** quilting, be sure to measure and trim the borders to your desired finish size.

For fabric requirements for adding this type of border to your blocks see page 43.

The finished quilt with its built-in outer border.

Here the black fabric has been cut into wonky borders and added to the square block.

Adding Wonky Block Borders

Adding wedges to your blocks instead of straight border strips will create a "wonky" setting for each block. This can be a lot of fun because it is very forgiving in terms of measurement, cutting, and sewing. If you are the type of quilter who values fun over precision, give this a try!

Read through the process before beginning to see how you might want to customize it for your quilt. Remember, these are not rules, just guidelines to help you finish.

First, measure your blocks. Then decide if you want all one color for your wedges and joining strips or if you want to go scrappy. For the project shown, I chose to use black wedges and black joining strips to let the original blocks stand out. You can use any solid, print or scraps; it's your choice.

Next, **cut rectangles that are slightly longer than one side of your block and 4″ wide**. Cut the same number of rectangles as the number of blocks you have.

My blocks in the photos are 8½″ square and my wedges are 4″ x 9½″. If you are working with much larger blocks, add 1½″ or 2″ to the length of your blocks.

Next, divide your rectangles into stacks easily divisible by the number of blocks you have. I had 20 blocks so I made 5 stacks of 4 rectangles each. Now cut across the stacks to make the wedges that will border two sides of your blocks. A few tips:

- as you make the angle cuts in the stacks of wedges, keep the stacks separate
- don't cut corner to corner; leave at least ¾″ from the corners
- vary the angles of your cuts on each stack, from sharp to almost straight

Keeping your stacks of wedges paired up and apart from each other, gather your blocks for sewing. Match the wedges made from one rectangle to one block, sewing the wedges to opposite sides of the block, right sides of the fabric together. Be sure to **sew the diagonal (bias) edge of the wedge to the block.** Leave some excess wedge off both ends of the block rather than lining up one end of the wedge with an edge of the block.

Sew the first set of wedges to the opposite sides of the block.

When all of the first set of wedges are sewn onto your blocks, press the blocks with the seams going toward the wedges. Trim the excess bits off so that the wedges are straight with the block.

Next, measure the longest edges of your new blocks and cut a new set of rectangles to match that length. Cut the same number of rectangles as you have blocks. On these blocks I ended up with about 11½″ edges at their longest. I decided to round up and cut my next set of rectangles 12″ x 4″.

This next step is important: **Cut the angles of your second set of wedges using roughly the same angles as your first set of wedges,** keeping them in stacks just like you did with your first set of wedges.

When sewing your second set of wedges to each block, try to match the angles of the first set of wedges with the angles of the second set.

The reason for this is to keep the balance of fabric and prevent large gaps that reduce your total block size. I didn't do this with my first set of blocks and had to go back and add fabric to some blocks. It's better to match the **wedge angles** as you sew them on. They don't need to match perfectly; they should just be close. Again, sew the diagonal edge of the wedge to the block.

After the second set of wedges is sewn on, press seams toward the wedges. You're ready to move on to Layering and Quilting. Remember, **don't trim the blocks yet.** They may look a little too wonky, but that's just fine for now.

For fabric requirements for adding a wonky border to your blocks see page 43.

Sew the second set of wedges, cut at a similar angle as the first.

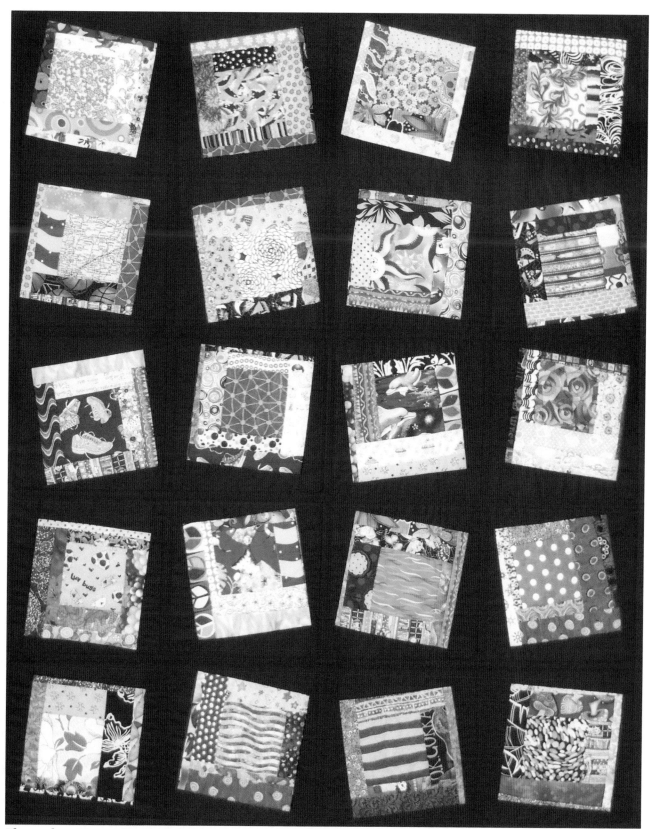

The wonky setting and black block borders and joining strips are perfect for these colorful, scrappy blocks.

Setting Your Blocks On Point

The "on−point" setting is one of the loveliest in quilting, in my opinion, especially for blocks that have a sort of direction, as with leaves. The surrounding fabric becomes a significant part of the quilt and could possibly overpower the blocks because there's so much of it. Be sure to lay your blocks on the fabric to see how the final quilt will look. This setting will also make your quilt quite a bit larger than a straight setting would so it's perfect if you have just a few quilt blocks.

You'll need a lot of fabric for this type of setting, and it's important that the fabric not be directional. The joining strips are going to cross through the "setting" triangles, and you will probably want those strips to just blend in, not stand out.

To create an on−point setting, for our purposes, you will add large overlapping triangles to every side of the block. To do this, cut block border squares the exact same size as your block; you'll need twice as many block border squares as you have quilt blocks. Then cut those squares once, from corner to corner, creating oversized triangles.

Cut the block border squares to the same size as your quilt squares. Then cut the squares corner to corner.

Center the triangles on one edge of a quilt block and sew.

55

When sewing on the first set of triangles, center them with your blocks, leaving equal amounts overhanging on either edge of the blocks.

After sewing two triangles to opposite sides of each block, press the seams toward the triangles and trim the excess bits off the ends of the triangles.

Sew the remaining triangles on, and press. Your blocks are now ready for layering and quilting. Remember, **don't trim or square up the blocks now**.

When your blocks are quilted and ready for trimming, it's important to center the block, not the surrounding fabric, under the ruler before trimming the edges.

Make sure that the points are evenly aligned under your ruler, top to bottom and side to side. This gives the quilt a nicely finished line, even though the block points don't meet, as they would with a traditional on-point setting.

For fabric requirements for adding this type of border to your blocks see page 43.

You can see here that the on—point setting uses much more fabric than the other block borders discussed in this chapter.

3. Layering

In this section, I'll share my best techniques for cutting batting, preparing and cutting backing fabrics, layering and pinning your quilt blocks in preparation for quilting them.

The very best part of this process is that every single block is a little quilt!

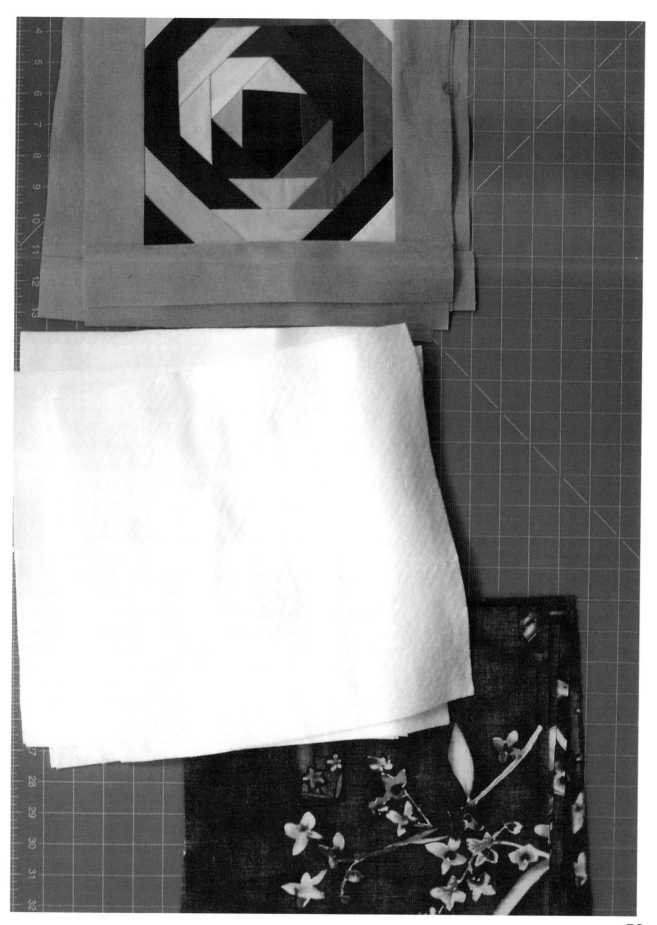

Prepare the Backing

If you haven't already chosen a backing fabric, go back to the Planning chapter and take a look at the photos of the backs of the quilts to view some options that you might not have considered.

Remember, there are many options for your quilt back. It can be all one fabric, including the joining strips, perhaps a large print. You could reverse some of the blocks on the top of your quilt as a design element, bringing the backing to the top and the blocks to the back, making a truly reversible, unified quilt. You could use a fabric that's featured on the top of the quilt, for a color–coordinated look, or a completely opposite color scheme.

When I make quilts that use scraps on the top, I love using scrap fabrics on the back. On other quilts I love the chance to use all one fabric as my backing, usually a fabric that I've totally fallen in love with.

If you haven't already, **press and starch your backing fabric**, before cutting it. This step is a tremendous help when cutting, layering and machine quilting on a home sewing machine. See the Planning chapter for tips on starching.

Keep in mind that if you pre-washed your blocks or top fabrics, and not the backing fabric, they may shrink differently, giving you a more puckered look than you anticipate.

Remember, you're cutting backing squares for your individual blocks. Although I can be pretty frugal with fabric, I've learned not to cut the backing squares too small. If I have enough fabric to do it, I prefer 1″ excess all the way around the block. So if my block (with block borders) measures 10″, I'll cut my backing squares to 12″. I've been short on fabric in the past, and tried using just ½″ excess on the backing squares, but it created problems when machine quilting near the edge of the blocks.

When cutting my backing out of yardage, I normally cut only the squares that I need, from along the selvage edge, leaving a long strip of whatever's left at the fold. I often used this leftover strip of fabric for the *block joining strips* on the back of my quilt. For more about cutting fabric for the joining strips, see page 94.

For this quilt I used left-over fabrics from the top of the quilt and brown yardage (which was also used for the binding) arranged in a checkerboard.

For this quilt backing and joining strips, I used one large print fabric. You can barely tell where the blocks and rows are joined, yet I didn't do anything special when cutting the fabric or joining the blocks and rows.

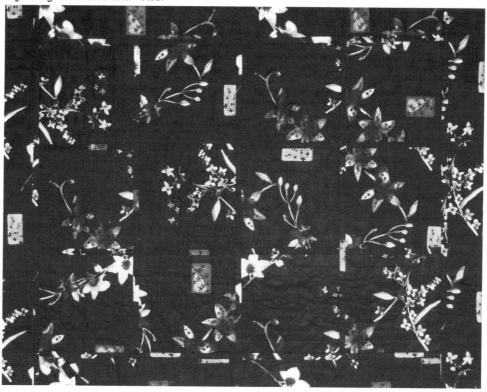

Prepare the Batting

I prefer to use the flattest, stiffest batting possible, and I've had great results with Warm & Natural and Warm & White batting. The reason I like it is the same reason that I like my fabrics starched: stiff fabrics and stiff batting mean easier handling while machine quilting and joining the blocks. The stiffness washes out of both the batting and the fabrics. Also, I find this brand of batting has a certain "grip" to it that helps when smoothing the layers for pinning and quilting.

Cut your batting squares the same size or just slightly smaller than your **backing fabric squares**. You can use packaged batting or leftover scraps of batting.

I usually buy batting on the roll, and I cut it first into strips, using scissors, then into squares, using a 60mm cutter and large acrylic ruler (20½" x 20½"). To cut strips, mark a line on the batting (sliding the ruler sideways across the batting as you go) and then cut along that line with scissors. Then stack the strips and cut squares with the rotary cutter.

The batting that you choose will impact the density of your quilting. Some batting can be quilted with up to 8" of space between quilting stitches, while other batts require stitching every 2".

If you don't follow the manufacturer's instructions for the density of recommended quilting, you could end up with wads of batting inside your quilt once the quilt is washed.

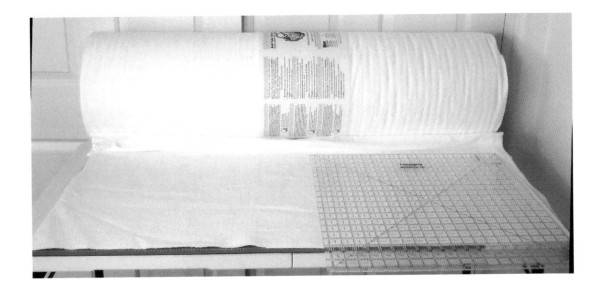

Layer the batting strips on top of each other and cut the squares, starting at the raw edge and working toward the fold. I cut 4-6 layers of batting at a time with my large square ruler. This is where the larger cutter comes in so handy! You can use this same method for packaged batting, or you can cut your squares individually, whatever is most comfortable to you. I cut my batting squares individually for years before I became brave enough to try cutting through six layers at a time. The batting squares don't have to be precisely measured; they just need to be larger than your blocks by about 1″ all the way around.

Layering and Smoothing

The two most important things to remember when layering your backing, batting and quilt blocks:

- *Keep the backing fabric right side down*

- *Smooth the layers of block-batting-backing multiple times.*

This ensures that you won't have problems with puckers or wrinkles while you are quilting your blocks.

The process of layering the backing, batting and the blocks, then smoothing and pinning, is very relaxing for me. When I have my stack of blocks pinned, I know that within just a few hours I'll have a finished quilt, and that's why I love this step. It's also the first time that I can feel my quilt coming together. The three layers are now together; and it's starting to feel like a real quilt, not just a bunch of fabric sewn together.

Lay a backing square, with the fabric right side down, on the table in front of you. Place a batting square on the backing, smoothing out any wrinkles. Place a block on the batting, centering it on the batting.

Start smoothing with both hands at the center of the block, gently pressing down with the palm of your hands while sliding your hands toward opposite edges of the block. Don't use too much pressure, just enough to see that your hands are both pressing all the layers together and also smoothing out any wrinkles.

Plus sign motion, step 1.

Plus sign motion, step 2.

Plus sign motion, step 3.

Plus sign motion, step 4.

X motion.

Pinning with a Kwik Klip.

The process that I follow, for each block, is:

1. Place the backing right side down, center a square of batting and lay a block right side up.
2. Smooth on top using a "plus sign" motion.
3. Smooth on top using an "X" motion (from center to corner).
4. Flip the whole set over gently.
5. Smooth on the back using the same set of motions (this is the time to double check that the backing fabric is layered correctly with the right side of the fabric out).
6. Flip over, block side up, and give a couple more smoothing motions.
7. Pin the block.

When the block is pinned, I gently set it aside and start on the next one.

Pinning

With your space set up comfortably, map out a plan for the quilting on your blocks. The reason for doing this, before pinning, is so you don't put pins where you intend to quilt. It is far easier and faster to quilt around pins than it is to stop and take them out while quilting.

With your quilting plan in mind, put a pin every 4″ to 6″. I like using the back side of my cutting mat as a base, so that the pins don't damage the table or countertop or the top side of my mat.

I prefer curved #2 nickel pins, and I love to use a Kwik Klip to help close the pins. I learned to buy quality pins after I made the mistake of buying bargain bags of pins that came with a sticky residue on them, which made them almost impossible to push through the fabrics and batting. Nice sharp pins make this process so quick and easy.

If you choose to spray baste your blocks, be sure to follow all the manufacturer's instructions for safe use of the spray.

If you have already done your layout and your blocks have layout tags on them, move your layout tags to areas of the block that won't be quilted. Remove each while quilting that block and immediately pin it back on when done. More on the tags and quilt layout in the Joining chapter.

4. Quilting

The quilting process is easier than you can imagine because you're quilting small blocks.

I'll show you how to quilt with straight lines, curvy lines, decorative stitches, stitch-in-the-ditch and simple free-motion quilting.

Threads, presser feet, stops and starts, and more are covered here. Get ready to have some fun!

Machine Quilting Basics

Before you even choose the method of quilting that you want to use, let's go over a few basics of machine quilting. This section will be useful if you have never used a sewing machine to quilt a quilt before, and it's a good review if you've had problems with machine quilting or if you have used only one method of quilting in the past.

I like to plan out my quilting, using my finger to trace the design I want directly on the block, as if I were drawing the quilting design with my finger. That helps me "set" the quilting path in my mind. By finger tracing it, I now have a good idea of how I need to move the block around while quilting. I do this for both stitch-in-the-ditch quilting and for free-motion quilting.

If this is your first attempt at machine quilting, I suggest you choose something simple like a straight stitch or stitch-in-the-ditch, and do some practicing on scrap fabrics or a small panel.

After quilting your first block, if you find that you absolutely hate the quilting, I suggest that you stop, remove the stitching, and start over with a new quilting plan. I know that sounds drastic, but it's a lot better than being unhappy with your quilt forever. Take your time, take the stitches out, and look at other quilts in books, magazines, and online until you find a new idea for quilting your quilt.

Presser Feet and Pressure Settings

Having the right presser foot for your sewing machine and adjusting the **pressure setting** on the presser foot can make a big difference in how easy, or difficult, it can be to quilt by machine.

I very much believe in using the foot designed for particular types of sewing; it makes things much easier.

For decorative stitch quilting, you'll need your zigzag foot. This foot has a wider opening, so be sure to change the needle plate for wider stitching. For free-motion quilting, you'll use a darning foot, which usually has a circular or oval opening and a spring mechanism.

A walking foot, also called an "even feed foot," puts pressure on and moves the top fabric, just like the feed dogs do on the bottom fabric. Whenever possible, I

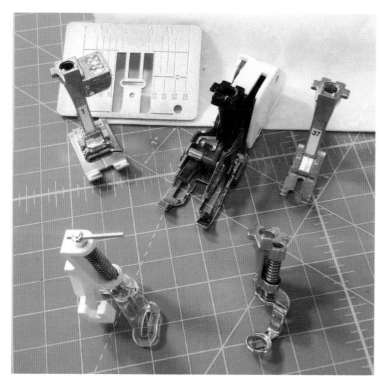

Clockwise, from top left: Needle plate with wide opening for decorative stitching and a wide-opening foot for zigzag quilting or decorative stitch quilting.

Walking foot for stitch-in-the-ditch quilting.

Quarter-inch foot for piecing.

Bottom: two open-toe darning or free-motion quilting feet.

prefer to use my walking foot for all straight stitching, including straight-stitch quilting. However you can use your normal straight-stitch foot if you choose.

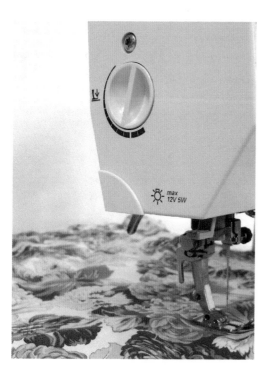

On this machine the pressure control is a dial on the side of the sewing machine head.

The pressure settings change how much pressure your sewing machine puts on the presser foot. Too much pressure creates waves, wrinkles, and puckers in the material. Too little pressure allows the fabric to move and slide around too much, creating an uneven stitching line.

Pressure setting adjustments can be found on many machines but not all. Check your sewing machine manual for where the adjustment mechanism is on your machine. On older machines, it's usually on the top of the machine; on newer machines (generally), it's on the side of the machine head.

69

Bringing up the Bobbin Thread

I ***always*** bring the bobbin thread to the top of the block before beginning any quilting. I recommend that you make this a regular practice. If you've ever had a machine "bind up with thread" or found a "thread nest" on the back of your quilt, you know what happens when you **don't** bring up the bobbin thread. That bobbin thread, left loose on the underside of your project, can wreak havoc with your quilt and your machine. *Avoid these problems by making it a habit to always bring the bobbin thread up through the quilt, to the top of your project.* The only exception is when I start at the edge of the quilt or block, in which case I hold the ends of **both** the top and bobbin threads.

There are two ways to bring up the bobbin thread. Here are the steps for the first method: position your quilt block where you want to begin quilting and, while holding the end of the top thread, take only one stitch. Lift the presser foot and move the block slightly so you can tug the top thread upward. Pull until you have a loop of bobbin thread big enough to grasp with your fingers, then gently tug until you've brought the loose end of the bobbin to the top of the quilt block. You can tell which end is the loose end by how much tension is on the thread. Move the quilt block back to the position it was in, with the bobbin thread coming up directly under the needle, and begin stitching, holding the ends of both threads.

Take a single stitch, then raise the presser foot. Holding the top thread, move the quilt block slightly. Tug the top thread until you see the loop of the bobbin thread. Pull on the bobbin thread, bringing the end up. Holding both threads, slide the quilt block back into place and lower your presser foot.

In the second method, take one stitch and, with the presser foot still down, tug gently on the top thread. You will see the loop of the bobbin thread pop up. Place a pin or stiletto through that bobbin thread loop, and gently pull the end of the thread up. Begin stitching while holding the ends of both threads.

Any way that you choose to do it, bring the bobbin thread up every time you begin to sew inside a block or quilt.

Starts and Stops

In garment sewing, we are taught to "back tack," which means taking 2-3 stitches forward, taking the same number of stitches backward and then sewing forward again to continue on with the seam. This secures the ends of the threads and keeps the seam from unraveling. It's very useful when making a garment, but it's almost never done while quilting. However, when machine quilting, you need to secure the ends of the threads to keep the quilting from coming undone. Otherwise you'll end up with lots of loose threads on your quilt.

There are several ways to secure the ends. Here are my two easiest:

Bring up the bobbin thread ¼″ away from where you want to start quilting, along the quilting path you intend to follow. Stitch in reverse toward the spot you want to begin quilting, *over the quilting path you intend to take.* This should only be 2-3 stitches. Stop and begin quilting forward sewing over the few stitches you just took, and keep on quilting. I call this "back up and go."

The second method is even easier. Simply hold your quilt block in place for 2-3 stitches. The machine will take the tiniest little stitches, or it will just stitch in place. Then begin your quilting. Those 2-3 stitches, taken almost on top of each other, will anchor the end of your quilting.

Follow the same process when ending a line of quilting, if you are not sewing off the edge of the block. There's no need to secure or tack the ends of your stitching lines if they go off the edge of your block because they will be secured by either the joining strips or the quilt binding.

My Best Machine Quilting Tips

Arrange your sewing area so that it fits you ergonomically. You should have a wide, flat surface to quilt on, at a height that suits your body. I can't emphasize this enough. A flat surface all around your sewing machine makes all the difference in the world when quilting a quilt on a home sewing machine.

It's also important to take regular breaks, to be seated in a comfortable chair, to have good lighting, and to give yourself many pats on the back as you finish each step on your way to finishing your quilt.

Density of Quilting

Personal taste is the deciding factor when it comes to density of quilting—meaning how close and tight the quilting is—and how much quilting you can see on a quilt. Personal tastes in quilting are as different for people as their tastes in color and design.

Please keep this in mind as you evaluate the photographs and decide what methods and designs to use for **your** quilting.

Ask yourself, "Is there enough quilting on this block?" as you look at each photo. If you are not happy with the quilting on your block, but you can't quite put your finger on exactly why, it's probably because there's not enough quilting for your taste.

This block is strongly quilted with stitch-in-the-ditch quilting, yet none of it is visible. Is that enough quilting for your tastes?

I find that it's almost impossible to "over quilt" something of your own. You know when to stop when you see it. But I often see quilters who are unhappy with the quilting that's been done on their quilts. When I suggest adding a little bit more, they perk right up with, "Yes, that's exactly what I'd like to see!"

If you are unsure of your own tastes, look through quilt books, and magazines, at quilt shows, and at your local quilt shop to observe the quilting on all the quilts. So often we just look at the quilt design; however, once you start looking at the actual quilting, you'll be a lot clearer about what you like.

If you can, practice on a panel or other pre-printed fabric and test out various densities, to see how they feel. When you touch a finished quilt, you are feeling the fabric, the batting, and the quilting.

Keep in mind that whatever quilting you do on your blocks will be seen on the back of your quilt. This is particularly important if you've chosen a backing fabric that you want to stand out, and you use a contrasting bobbin thread for your quilting.

This block has both stitch-in-the-ditch quilting and free-motion stippling. The dense stippling makes the star pattern really stand out.

Other Tips

When machine quilting, there are a few tools that can make things easier. Many quilters find it helpful to wear gripper type gloves. Alternatives to gloves are rubber fingertips, gripping pads, and horseshoe–shaped grippers.

Clean and oil your machine as needed before starting your quilting, removing all lint from the race and bobbin area. Change needles so that you have a nice sharp needle. Be sure you are using a thread made for machine quilting not hand quilting. There are many varieties of threads available: cottons, rayons, polyesters, and combinations of cotton and polyester. If you've had issues with thread breakage in the past, switch over to a polyester or cotton–wrapped polyester thread. These threads have more "give" than cotton, and sometimes just that little bit of difference can help a lot.

Knowing what you like to see and feel in a quilt gives you a strong sense of direction when it comes to machine quilting.

You will find it much easier to select quilting designs for your quilts once you have defined your tastes.

In the past, you may have seen quilt designs you thought looked nice and wanted to make, but you were put off by the quilting shown on the pattern.

*I encourage you to look past that and envision that quilt pattern with quilting done the way **you** like.*

Types of Quilting

Quilting can be done in so many ways. Here are the seven options I use most.

Stitching-in-the-Ditch

"Stitch-in-the-ditch," often abbreviated as SID, is a quilting technique that puts the straight-stitch quilting right in the seam lines of the block, making them almost invisible. When the quilt is washed, you won't even see the quilting lines.

Stitch-in-the-ditch is easy and, with a little bit of planning, goes very quickly.

If you love quilts for the fabrics in them and don't care for a lot of thread work or quilting covering your beautifully pieced block, stitch-in-the-ditch is the technique to use.

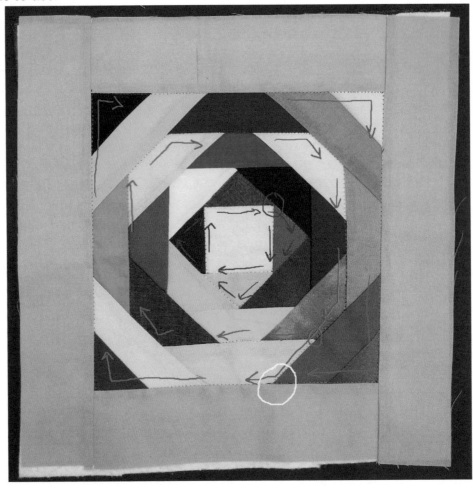

By planning my quilting path, I was able to quilt this Pineapple Log Cabin by stopping and starting only twice.

Sewer's Aid helps clear polyester thread run through your sewing machine easily.

If you truly don't want your quilting to show, I recommend using a clear **polyester thread** (not nylon) on top and a cotton thread in the bobbin. If your sewing machine is at all finicky about the polyester thread, apply a light coating of Sewer's Aid to the spool.

When stitching in the ditch, I like to map out the exact path I am going to take with my stitching, preferably one with few stops and starts. If possible, I like to start in the center of the block and keep turning the block as I work my way toward the outer edge of the block.

In the Pineapple Log Cabin on the opposite page, I started where the red circle is and quilted, continuously, lifting the presser foot only to turn corners (with the needle down). When I arrived back at my start point, I turned the quilt slightly and continued sewing, moving to the next square. I finished at the same spot, but I quilted two inner squares in the process.

Next I cut threads and began again where the blue circle is (lower right–hand corner), again sewing around one square then jumping out to the next square. This time I ended at the spot where the yellow circle is. By choosing each start point carefully, you can make several passes around the block without stopping to break threads and start over.

Whenever possible, I use my walking foot for stitching in the ditch, with the feed dogs up and medium to medium-light pressure setting on the presser foot. You can use a regular straight-stitch foot, also, instead of a walking foot.

Straight Line Quilting

I love, love, love straight-line quilting. It's fast, traditional, simple, and there's no fear involved. You can literally do it with your eyes closed, especially if you have a walking foot.

You can sew straight lines in pairs, narrow or wide, in a large or small checker-board grid, or whatever you like, and as your batting allows.

I like to mark the edges of my blocks with dots using a fabric–safe pencil, and then just sew from dot to dot. You could use your fabric–safe marker to draw the whole line if you want, too. Just remember that the goal is not perfection, and no one is ever going to whip out a ruler to see if your lines are slightly off the mark.

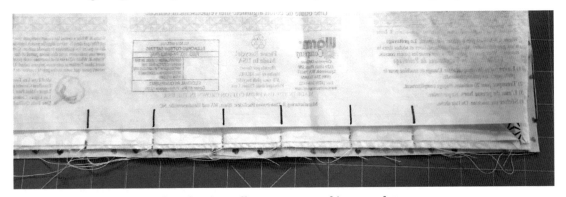

Here I used the paper around my batting roll to create a marking template.

In the above photo, I used a piece of scrap paper to establish the width between lines. You could use your acrylic quilting ruler, freezer paper, or gridded paper, too. In this case, I cut my scrap paper to the size of my blocks and used it to mark two sides of every block. I then straight stitched from dot to dot on each block. It went fast!

When I am done with all the straight lines going across each block, I mark each block over again, on the opposite sides. I then sew in that direction, from dot to dot again, to get a full grid across each block.

When sewing straight lines, it helps to always start on the same edge, sewing in the same direction with every line. Also, as you sew the second set of lines (the "crossing" lines), you will most likely have small puckers where the lines intersect. This is not because you are doing anything wrong; it's just the nature of quilting. If the puckers are large, and you think you might have too much pressure on your presser foot, make a slight adjustment to lighten the pressure. If you take too much pressure off, however, your block will "wobble" as you sew and you won't get a straight line.

I very much enjoy the look of the gridded quilting, so I change the normal stitch length setting on my machine to a slightly longer one, to allow the stitches to be seen better. If you use a test scrap, you can play with your stitch-length settings until you find one that you like. If you have an electronic machine, one that re-sets every time you turn it on, be sure to make note of the stitch-length setting you are using and keep it handy until your quilting is finished. On the red-and-white quilt below I used a setting of 8 stitches per inch. On the quilt featured on page 46, I used a 12—weight variegated thread and set my machine for 7 stitches per inch.

Expect tiny puckers when quilting a grid. They will be un-noticeable after the quilt is washed.

Curved Line Quilting

A very fun way of quilting is with curved lines, using a walking foot. Like wandering down a sandy beach, your stitch lines will be visible, inconsistently spaced, and give a feeling of movement and freedom.

Because I like to control how much curve goes into my lines, I either place my hands flat on the block, or I grip the side edges of the block, like I would grip a steering wheel. Then I gently swing the block slowly side to side as it moves away from me under the needle.

I like to do a few lines of curved quilting on the block borders. Then, after joining blocks into a row (and using a straight stitch to secure the top joining strip), I add one or two more curved lines down the inner borders, where the blocks have been joined together, crossing over the joining strip.

Curved lines are perfect for quilting on block borders.

The quilting lines will not match up from block to block unless you make a quilting template or mark your blocks. The quilting won't go over the joining strips unless you do some additional quilting **after** joining your blocks.

To do this, add some quilting after joining your blocks into rows, and you can also add quilting after joining your rows into a quilt.

In these blocks, that have been joined with white fabric, the curvy quilting stays nicely inside the blocks.

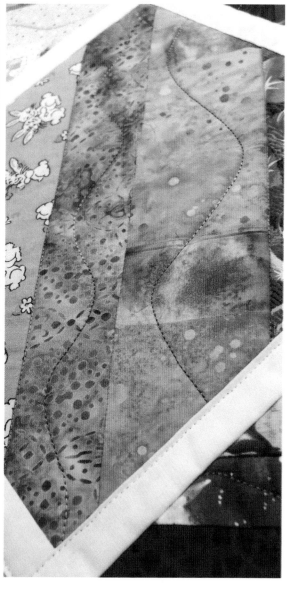

The horizontal quilting lines on the individual block borders don't connect, but the vertical quilting lines, added after the blocks were joined together, serve to visually connect the two blocks and further hide the joining strips.

Decorative Stitch Quilting

Use your zigzag or decorative stitch foot (not your walking foot) for this technique, which looks good on any quilt and looks especially good on scrap quilts. This is a wonderful opportunity to use the lovely decorative stitches that come with many sewing machines! You can stitch following the seam lines, slightly off to one side of the seam lines, or straight across the block, whatever you like best.

Decorative stitches look so elegant when done with a rayon thread. If you choose to use a decorative thread, like rayon, as a top thread, consider using a cotton or a cotton–wrapped polyester thread of a similar color in the bobbin. I find that using a slick thread on the top and in the bobbin can create issues when trying to secure the stitches. Be sure to bring up the bobbin thread when starting a line of stitching inside your block. When doing small segments of stitching, I recommend starting in the center of the block and stitching toward the edge. If you use many different colored threads, add a little bit of stitching to each block with one thread, then change threads and start over, adding more stitching to each block. Continue for as many threads as you want to use, until all blocks are quilted.

If you have pressed all your block seams to one side while making your blocks, you may want to steer clear of using the highly complicated stitches along your seams. These stitches work best on flat fabric and blocks where the seams have been pressed open.

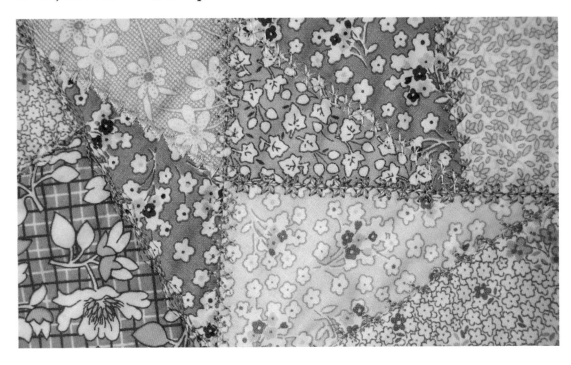

Echo Quilting

This type of quilting looks very nice on appliqué blocks and T–shirt quilts. It can be done free-motion or with a walking foot, if the pressure is not too heavy and the curves are not too sharp.

The easiest way to do echo quilting is to start around the edge of the appliqué and slowly spiral out, in one long continuous line. If your appliqué is placed so that it isn't possible to do one long line, try doing half the block at a time, quilting right off the edge of the block.

Placement of the lines for echo quilting is all in the eye of the quilter. You can have as little as ¼″ space between lines or 1″ or more; it's entirely up to you.

The echo quilting on this piece is quite dense, at less than ¼″ apart, because I really wanted the center to stand out.

Free-Motion Stippling

Free-motion machine quilting is done with the feed dogs down, using a darning or free-motion foot. The idea is that you move the quilt block any way you want, stitching a freely as you like. The stitch length and the density of the quilting is all up to you and how you move your blocks.

Take a close look at the small stitches at the star points below. When stipple quilting a block like the one below, I begin quilting in one corner of a white square and stitch to the opposite corner, covering the area in swirls, loops, and squiggles, working my way to my "exit corner." There I slow down my sewing speed and take a few tiny stitches to cross over into the next area that I want to quilt. Using this method, I have only one start and one stop for machine quilting the entire block.

Notice the stitching around the triangle points, connecting the stippling in the white fabric areas?

Yes, it's okay to cross over your stitching lines. Just have fun!

The idea is to quilt your quilt any way you want in the easiest way possible. If a "don't cross lines rule" has kept you from free-motion quilting, *I hereby give you permission to cross your lines and ignore any other rules, too.*

If you've never tried free-motion quilting, practice on a muslin square or a simple panel. And most of all, relax. It's not open heart surgery; it's only quilting. No one's going to take a magnifying glass to your quilt.

I highly recommend using a cotton-wrapped polyester core thread for free-motion quilting because it has a bit of a stretch to it that is very forgiving. I love to use gloves while free-motion quilting for added grip and easy control of the block while moving it around.

Combination Quilting

I will often combine both stitch-in-the-ditch quilting with some other type of quilting on my blocks—either free-motion or curved lines. When I know that this is my plan, I do all of the stitch-in-the-ditch quilting first, on all of my blocks. Then I go back and do whatever additional quilting I want on each block.

When I have a block that has a design element that I want to highlight, I'll often stitch-in-the-ditch around the pattern and then do more dense quilting in the rest of the block. Remember, density of quilting is a personal decision, and it's important for you do choose quilting designs and density that suits you.

Trimming

Once you have done as much quilting on your blocks as you want, it's time to trim each of them down to an exact, uniformly sized, square.

I'll outline two ways of doing this, but you may have your own way. No matter what, **it's essential that the blocks be all the same size and be square**. It's actually easy to cut them in a way that *isn't* square, so that's why I emphasize the need for squareness here.

If your blocks have a symmetrical inner pattern, such as an on-point setting or a built-in border setting, it's important to balance your "trimming for squareness" with the actual block pattern inside the borders and with the desired finished borders. If you used the wonky style of adding block borders, you'll need to account for the degree of tilt you want for the inner block as you squarely trim the block.

First measure all of your blocks using the top fabric as your guide, not the batting or backing. Find the smallest block and make sure that it is large enough to be trimmed to the size you want for your quilt.

If there's a huge difference between the sizes, and the smallest block is not the finished size you want, consider adding fabric onto the smaller blocks to make them larger. However, my best advice is to just trim all blocks down to your smallest size and throw the trimmings into your scrap basket for use on your next scrap quilt.

The wonky blocks tend to have the most ragged edges. Make sure you find the smallest one before beginning the trimming process. Otherwise, you'll find yourself trimming twice or having to add to the smallest block.

The steps for trimming each block are as follows:

1. Align the ruler(s) with any inner block designs.
2. Check that there's plenty of excess to trim off the sides *opposite* the sides you're trimming.
3. Check that the inside "square" mark is on the quilt block fabric, not the batting or backing.
4. For built-in border blocks, be sure that you are trimming the block borders to match the finished widths you desire.
5. Trim two sides and gently rotate the block.
6. Check that the inner corner as well as the outside edges are exactly at the mark for your size block. It's easy to make a "not square" cut by checking only the outside edges and not the inner corner (*see photo at the bottom of page 86*).

The second set of cuts is only for fully squaring up the block, *not for balancing the inner quilt block.*

The easiest way to trim blocks is with a ruler that is larger than the block; that's why I love both my 15″ and 20½″ square rulers. When trimming, whether you're using one ruler or two, it's okay to move your hand on the ruler; just lift up without moving the ruler and replace your hand where it's most comfortable.

If you are using two rulers, slide the smaller ruler up and down the side of the larger ruler, making sure the inner block is square and that you have the full finished size of your block available for cutting.

It can be slightly time consuming to be this cautious when trimming, but it's going to help a lot when you join your blocks. Having nicely squared blocks means you are going to have a nicely balanced, square quilt, and the joining process will be smooth and easy.

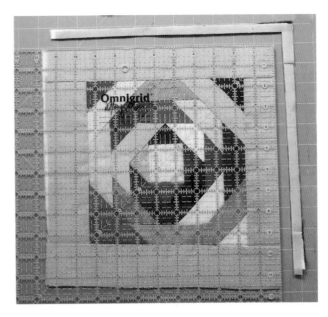

Check that the full block size can be cut from your block and that there's plenty of excess for trimming.

Center your inner block, making sure that the outer border is the correct width on the top and right-hand sides. Make sure there's **more** than the desired finished width for the outer border on the left-hand side and the bottom of the block.

Holding the ruler steady, cut the right-hand side and the top edge of the block. If you need to move your hand on the ruler, don't move the ruler. If you do, re-center it, checking all sides.

Lift your ruler and rotate your block gently. Replace the ruler and **check in three places to make sure your block stays square**: the upper left measurement, the lower left corner, and the bottom right.

All the edges of your block should show the same number, the size you want your blocks to be.

Trim the last two sides.

Follow the same process if using two rulers, sliding the smaller ruler along the edge of the larger ruler to ensure straightness of the inner block and full squareness of the block when making the first two cuts.

When you are sure you are trimming square, slide the small ruler to the top of the block and trim two sides.

Gently rotate the block.

Do the same to check the three points before making the second set of cuts.

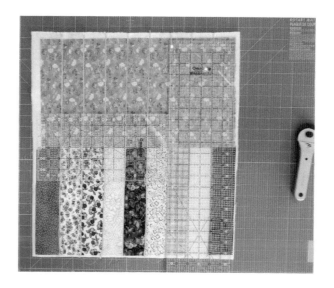

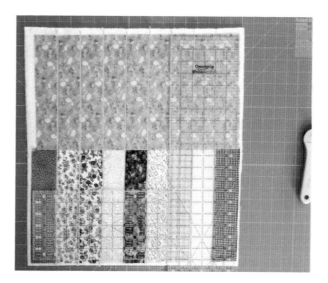

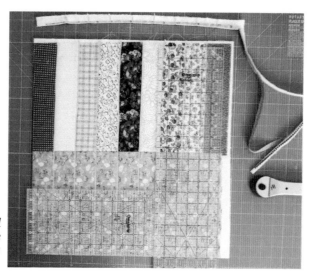

This block has been trimmed on two sides and rotated. Follow the same process of sliding the ruler to check for squareness before making the last two cuts.

5. Joining

Now that you are working with quilted blocks, do you feel how wonderful your quilt will be? Can you imagine it wrapped around you?

This is the stage that gets quilters really excited because your project goes from blocks to a quilt so very quickly. Each step has you excited to do the next one!

The process of joining your quilted blocks entails choosing a layout, joining the blocks into rows, and joining the rows into a quilt.

It goes *much faster* than you would imagine!

Note that the numbering starts on the right, with the number 1.

Choosing Your Quilt Layout

This is one of the most fun parts of making your quilt! Ask friends, family, other quilters, and anyone you want for advice and help; if you have small children who want to help, even better.

The idea behind the layout is to arrange your blocks in the way you would like to see them in the finished quilt. Then you'll tag each block with a small label so that, as you join blocks, you maintain the layout design that you chose.

If you have a design wall that you can put your blocks up on, that's great. I also use the living room floor or a bed. Use whatever works for you and have fun arranging your blocks.

Some blocks are so similar that I don't even pay attention to the block placement (for example my Pineapple Log Cabin). Other quilts have a directional backing, with a fairly generic top, like the Scrappy Stars, so the layout is done using the *back* of the quilt. No matter what determines the layout the labels are still pinned to the front of the blocks.

Label the blocks so the top row is "A" and the numbering starts on the right. Your upper right hand block is A1, the block to the left of that is A2 and so on. The block below A1 is B1 and directly below B1 is C1. All the blocks on the right-hand edge are a sequential letter of the alphabet, and all are #1. The numbers increase toward the left in each row.

Safety pin the label near the upper right hand corner of each block, about 2″ from the edge. You will sew the joining strips to the edges of most of the blocks, so you will need a few inches of space free around the edges for sewing them on.

Joining Your Blocks

Joining the blocks can be, at first, a little confusing. Basically, you are going to use a set of joining strips (one strip for the top and one for the back) to connect your blocks into rows and use a similar set of strips to join the rows into a quilt.

The joining strips are often not cut from the same fabrics. The top joining strip may match your block fabrics on top and the back joining strip may match the quilt backing fabrics.

The specific directions that I give in this section are here because they offer the best and easiest results. However, no two people sew, pull, stretch, press or even cut exactly the same way. I've seen this over and over in classes while teaching. The measurements I offer are my best guidelines, but they are not written in stone. You can change them to suit you! Yes, you have my permission to do so!

Once you have read through the process, my best suggestion is to make two little quilted scrap blocks, about 4" square, and then join them together, with scrap fabric.

This lets you understand the process and offers you a chance to change anything about it before you begin on your quilt blocks.

If it seems confusing, follow the instructions step by step (on faith) and you will have an "aha!" moment when your little scrap blocks come together.

The important thing to understand about the joining strips is that they act as both connectors and stabilizers to your quilt blocks. When cut on the lengthwise grain, your joining strips will not stretch. This helps keep your blocks square and your rows even as you join them together.

No part of quilt making is absolutely perfect and that includes the joining process. After you've made two or three quilts this way, you may develop a rhythm that gives you near-perfect results. But I always prefer to look at the big picture—finished is better than perfect, and a finished quilt is better than any amount of procrastination in the search for perfection.

The process of joining the blocks uses a series of utility stitches (straight stitch) and then a "finishing stitch" that often uses a thread that matches or complements the joining strip fabrics.

If you are fortunate enough to have two sewing machines and you choose to use a decorative stitch to secure your joining strips, it can be wonderfully helpful to set up one machine for straight stitching and the other for decorative stitching.

Here's the order of sewing:

1. Sew on block joining strips and join blocks into rows (straight stitch/regular thread).
2. Stitch down the top strip between the blocks (often a decorative stitch and/ or specialty thread).
3. Sew on row joining strips and join rows (straight stitch/regular thread).
4. Stitch down top row joining strips (decorative stitch and/or specialty thread).
5. Sew on binding (straight stitch/regular thread).
6. Sew binding to front of quilt (decorative stitch and/or specialty thread).

As you can see, if you are using one sewing machine, you could be changing feet and threads three times. But don't worry, I've made it sound more complicated than it really is!

These two blocks have been joined, but the top joining strip has not yet been sewn down. The blocks lay snugly next to each other, neither overlapping nor with a gap between them.

Cut the Binding Strips First

If you are going to use the same fabric for both the binding and row joining strips, let's talk a bit about cutting and economy of fabric. If this doesn't apply to you, skip this and go right into Cut the Joining Strips.

I often cut my binding strips before I cut any other fabrics, including my block borders. I am a strong believer in not wasting fabric, and I often match my binding to my block border and joining fabrics. By cutting the binding strips first, I have the longest possible yardage to work with, meaning that I will have to sew fewer seams to join the strips together to have enough for my binding.

There's only one exception to this process and that's when I am making a quilt with 20 blocks or more. Then it's easiest to cut off a single chunk of fabric for the block joining strips first, then cut binding strips and lastly row joining strips.

Before I cut, I fold my fabric several times lengthwise, so I'm able to cut through 2 yards of fabric at one time. Next, I cut the selvage off one edge. From there I cut as many binding strips as needed for the quilt. My binding is 2½″ wide and always cut on the lengthwise grain.

By folding the fabric several times lengthwise I was able to make one cut through 2 yards of fabric. What's left will be used for the block joining strips, block borders or setting triangles for the quilt blocks.

I recommend cutting the row joining strips next, then the block joining strips.

From left to right: binding, top row joining strip, back row joining strip, fabric for block joining strips, etc. The selvage, at the top, was cut off first.

94

Cut the Joining Strips

The joining strips are always the same width, even though the lengths depend on the size of your blocks and rows. **The top strips are 2″ wide and the back strips are 1¼″ wide** and both sets of strips are always cut on the lengthwise grain, which lets them act as stabilizers for your blocks.

It's important to cut your joining strips the exact length of your blocks and rows. It's easy to stretch the quilted blocks so, by matching your joining strips to the exact length of your blocks and rows, you maintain the squareness of your blocks, rows and your quilt.

Row Joining Strips

Count the number of rows in your quilt and subtract one. That's the number of row joining strip **pairs** you will need.

For example, if you have a quilt with 16 blocks, and your blocks are 15″ square, (4 blocks in a row, 4 rows in the quilt) you will need 3 strips that are 2″ x 60″ for row joining strips on the top and 3 strips that are 1¼″ x 60″ for row joining strips on the back. If you set aside some of your backing fabric for the back joining strips, now's the time to pull that out and cut it.

Often it turns out that I need an odd number of top row joining strips and I've cut one too many binding strips (because I cut them from folded fabric).

When this happens, I often trim down just one strip that was cut for binding to a become a row joining strip. If this doesn't make any sense yet, pass it by until you are actually calculating and cutting your binding and joining strips.

If you need to piece your row joining strips from smaller strips, follow the same instructions for joining binding strips in the Binding chapter.

Block Joining Strips

Count the number of blocks that you have in a row and subtract one. Multiply that number times the number of rows in your quilt and you have the number of block joining strip **pairs** you need to connect blocks for your quilt.

For example, if you have a quilt with 16 blocks (4 blocks in a row, 4 rows in the quilt), and your blocks are 15″ square, you will need 12 strips that are 2″ x 15″ for block joining strips on the top and 12 strips that are 1¼″ wide by 15″ long for block joining strips on the back.

Pin the Block Joining Strips On

Set aside all #1 blocks until after all the block joining strips are sewn on. If you didn't do a layout because all your blocks are the same, set aside one block for each row that you have.

Pinning the joining strips to the blocks is a three step process that happens all at the same time, all on the right-hand edge of each remaining block.

1. Place the back joining strip against the back of the quilt, right sides together and aligned with the right-hand edge of the block.
2. Fold (don't press) the top joining strip, right sides out, lengthwise and align the raw edges of the strip with the right-hand edge of the quilt block.
3. Layer and pin all layers—folded top strip, block, and back strip—on the right-hand edge of the block, making sure that the ends are all even with each other.

Do this for of all of the blocks except the #1 blocks.

Please don't attempt to sew the strips on without pins.

It takes far less time and frustration to pin than it does to have to go back and remove stitches because the back strip folded in or wavered. This is especially true when it comes to joining the rows of your quilt. It's not so much about trying to be perfect in your sewing; it's about avoiding the frustration and disappointment that comes when you don't pin.

From the bottom up, the layers are: back joining strip (right side up), quilt block, folded top joining strip (right side out).

I've made over 30 quilts using these methods, and every time that I think I can cheat, and not pin, guess what happens? The back joining strip wanders and folds or puckers under the block as I am sewing.

If you want to cut steps out of the process, then pin only the back joining strip and skip pinning on the top strip. But my best advice is to take the time to pin all three layers.

Sew the Joining Strips Onto the Blocks

Before sewing the strips on, check the pressure on your presser foot. No matter what your normal setting is, you will probably need to lighten the pressure just a little. If the fabrics are making a big "wave" in front of the needle, you probably have too much pressure on the presser foot. This is covered in detail on page 69 of the Quilting chapter.

If you are an experienced quilter, you will have heard of using a "scant" ¼" seam for piecing; however, when you sew your joining strips on you, will be using a *fat ¼"* seam—almost 5/16". This is much wider than a scant ¼", so it takes some getting used to.

For your very first quilt, I suggest sewing on one set of joining strips, then joining that block to another block, just to get the seam allowances right for you and your machine. Remember, we're **sewing with a fat ¼" seam**. Once you have the seam allowances that make you happiest, mark it on your sewing machine with painter's tape or a commercial product that helps mark the seam allowance.

It's very easy to chain piece the process of sewing on the joining strips. Simply butt one end of a block up next to another and keep right on stitching. Try not to let the chain of blocks fall off the backside of your sewing table because the weight will distort your stitching.

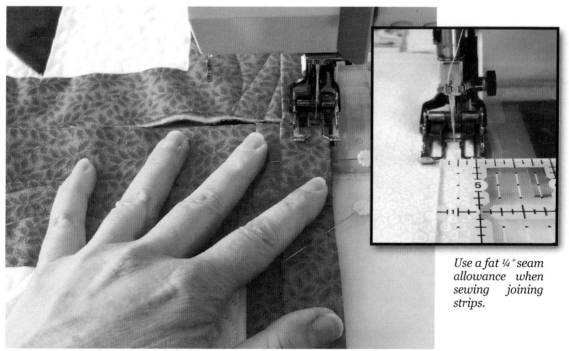

Use a fat ¼" seam allowance when sewing joining strips.

Block joining strips can be chain pieced.

Join the Blocks Into Rows

Now it's time to bring back your #1 blocks. You are going to join all the similarly **lettered** blocks into a row. You can choose to join your blocks in any order you want, joining A1 to A2, then A3 to A4, or you can just start adding on, joining A1 to A2, and then adding A3 to the A1-A2 group and so on.

My personal preference is to join the highest number blocks to each other, and then keep adding blocks, one at a time, to that row. So if my quilt has 5 blocks in a row, I join 5 to 4, then I add 3 to the edge of 4, I add 2 to the edge of 3, and lastly, I add 1 to the edge of 2. When I'm done with that letter row, I move on to the next row. I keep all the blocks on my left-hand side, never in the throat of the sewing machine. I don't pin the whole row first; I pin each block set just before I sew it.

Joining blocks into rows is a five step process.

1. Push and smooth the back joining strip away from the block with your fingers.
2. Align the raw edge of the left-hand side of one block to the raw edge of the back strip, with the back sides of the blocks together.
3. Make sure the block edges, top and bottom, are aligned.
4. Pin through the extended back joining strip and the block beneath it.
5. Sew the back joining strip to the block beneath it with a fat ¼″ seam.

Using block A1 and A2 as your first blocks to join, lay A2 face down (back of block facing up) or just fold it over, and finger press the back joining strip away from the block.

*With back sides together, align the **left** raw edge of A1 block with the raw edge of the back joining strip from A2 block.*

Be sure to line up the top and bottom edges of the blocks. Then pin.

Notice that the fabrics that are lined up are the (finger-pressed open) back joining strip on the top block and the edge of the bottom block.

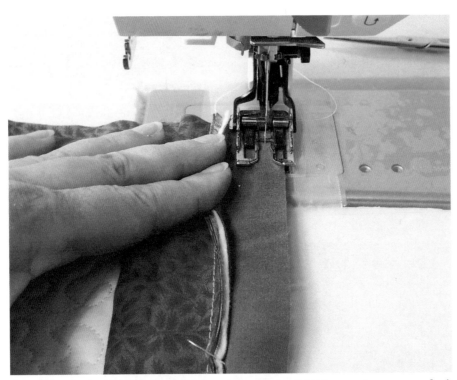

Sew along the inside of the back joining strip, using a fat ¼" seam. As you sew, don't let the bulky edge of the top block on the left push you off your seam line. If necessary, pull back on that seam to allow you to sew straight without interference.

When you have joined two blocks, cut threads and lay them flat. Both blocks should lay snugly against each other without overlapping and without a gap between them. If you do have a slight overlap, gently tug the blocks apart and see if that helps.

If you have a gap, you can close it up tight when you sew down the top joining strip, or you can go back now and re-sew the seam with a slightly wider seam allowance. You don't have to take out any stitches to do this, just sew a new, wider seam. Join the rest of your blocks into rows.

When joined, the blocks should lay snugly next to each other, with no overlap or gap between them.

Sew the Top Joining Strips Down

The one thing that is important to understand when sewing down the top joining strip is your stitches **may not** hit the back seam on the back of your quilt. There are ways to make it close, but I encourage you to not focus too much on this minor issue. It's as irrelevant as trying to bake dinner rolls that have the exact same level of "golden doneness" on the top of the roll as the bottom. The dinner rolls taste great no matter what, and your quilt will be gorgeous with or without some stitches hitting the back seam.

If you have been using utility piecing threads, now's the time to change. Select a bobbin thread that matches the back of your quilt and a top thread that either matches or enhances the top of your quilt.

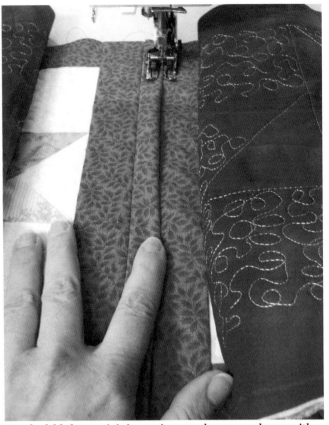
Gently fold the top joining strip over the gap and sew with a straight or decorative stitch.

Fold the top joining strip over the gap between the blocks and stitch down the folded edge. Don't pull it too much, just allow it to lay flat.

You can use a decorative stitch for this portion if you want. In this case I suggest matching thread colors for the top and bobbin. If you choose to use a decorative stitch to sew down the top strip, you may want to use one of the simpler stitches. Popular stitches are an elongated serpentine satin stitch and a narrow zigzag stitch.

For a faster finish, use a straight stitch.

You may choose to stitch on both sides of the strip or only on the folded side—it's your choice!

When using decorative stitches, make sure the quilt is perfectly flat, with excess quilt bunched up along all sides of the foot. This allows the sewing machine to move the quilt side-to-side, and forward and back, with no resistance.

To prevent the few difficulties that I've experienced when using decorative stitches on the top joining strips:

- use a stitch width of no more than 7mm wide and of medium or simple intricacy—wider or very intricate stitches can be distorted by the bulk of the seam.
- don't let the quilt hang off the edge of your sewing table—the stitches may be distorted because the weight of the quilt can pull on the area being stitched
- avoid a stitch that repeatedly sews in the same spot—the thread will sometimes break

Pin the Row Joining Strips On

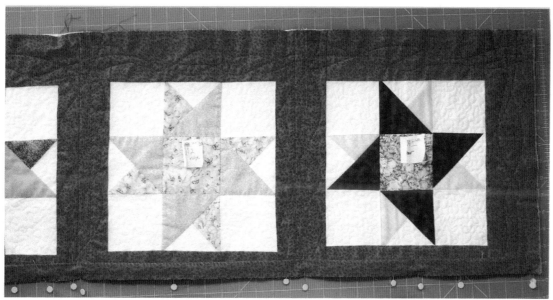

Pinning heavily helps keep your joining strips even and in place while you sew.

The process of joining rows is very similar to that of joining blocks. Try to use a long, flat surface that's comfortable to work on, and lay the entire row flat as you pin. For smaller quilts, you could use a flat table or ironing board, with a cutting pad on it. If the quilt is large, try combining several portable tables or use the floor.

First, set aside the bottom row, just like you set aside the #1 blocks. Next, pin the joining strips to the bottom edge of the remaining rows, exactly the same way as you pin the blocks. Pin heavily!

I recommend pinning the back joining strip on first, then flip the row over and pin on the top joining strip, leaving the first set of pins in place. It's a lot of pinning, but it's worth it, and it goes fairly quickly.

Start by pinning the end of the joining strip to the end of a row. Then smooth all three layers flat, and pin the center of the row. If there's excess fabric, make sure that it's even on both sides of that center pin. If you have to stretch the blocks a little to make the lengths match, stretch them evenly on both sides of the center pin. If the block row is longer than the joining strip, ease the excess in the same way.

Do you realize you're almost finished with your quilt at this point? Just join rows and put on binding, and it's done!

Next, working on just half of the row, pin that center (it's really the ¼ mark of the row). Check that everything's even on both sides of that center pin and continue to "pin centers" until the entire row is pinned.

Switch your sewing machine back to piecing threads, and sew the row joining strips on. If you've pinned well, you'll have an exact even match of joining strips and blocks at the beginning and end. If you end up with a difference of more than ⅛″, you should take your stitches out and start over, as the quilt won't come together right.

Join the Rows Together

Using a large, flat area, lay row A right side down and finger press the back joining strip away from the blocks, exactly as you did with the blocks.

Flip row A right side up and lay it on top of row B (which is right side down) and align the **top edge** of row B to the raw edge *of the back joining strip* on row A.

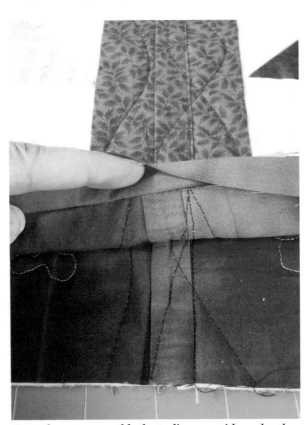

To make sure your blocks to line up with each other from row to row, start pinning at the intersections of the block joining strips, making sure that they are aligned. Peek between the row layers to do this.

Once all of these "intersections" are pinned, pin the rest of the rows together, making sure they match up evenly from end to end.

When sewing, I use my left hand to hold the row of blocks; my right hand is through the throat of my sewing machine, holding the row, guiding it and keeping it straight.

Be sure the fabric behind the needle is just as straight as the fabric in front of the needle. That helps keep a consistent and straight seam. Take it slowly and remember, you're almost done!

I prefer to join two rows together, then another two, and then join the halves of the quilt. If the quilt has five rows, I join two rows, and then join the other three into a group. Finally I sew one final seam up the middle, to join the two halves. I find it easiest to manage the bulk of the quilt that way, but you do whatever is comfortable for you. Join your rows exactly as you joined your blocks, with the same fat ¼″ seam.

I always take a little break between joining rows—almost a little celebration. When I can feel the quilt all rolled up and coming together, I know that it's just a few more seams away from being a real quilt, so I take my time and enjoy the process. Every single seam finished brings me one step closer to the finish line for that quilt, and I like to savor that feeling.

Lots of pins make sewing this seam much easier.

Use the tip of your pin to push the seams open.

Sew the Top Joining Strips Down

Switch back to your finishing threads and any special sewing machine foot that you might be using, and give your quilt as much table support as you can. Here's where you'll want to gather ironing boards and portable tables—anything that can give the quilt support while you do the last bit of stitching.

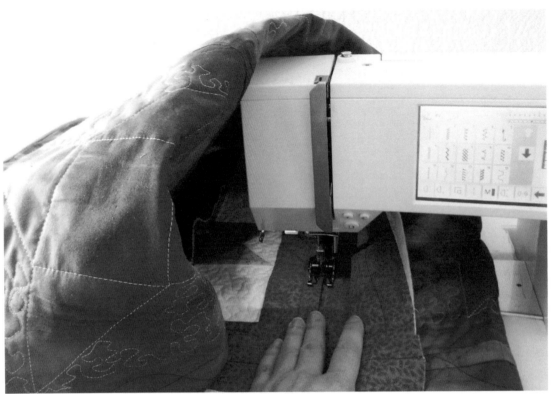

Try to keep the entire quilt flat and close to your sewing machine. Here I am sewing one of the outer rows on and there's only one row of quilt in the throat of the sewing machine.

To sew the inner row joining seams, I roll the quilt and secure the rolls. It helps a great deal, when you're trying to sew a straight line, to have control of your quilt. There are circular clips sold for this purpose, or you might think of a better way. The most important thing is this: Use a method that is **comfortable** for you that allows the machine to stitch evenly.

I prefer to sew the seams at the top and bottom of the quilt first, turning the quilt so that the bulk of it is on the left-hand side. Once those are done, it's time to tackle the inner seams closer to the middle of the quilt.

If your sewing machine table backs up to a wall, use the "hood" method of pulling the finished portion up and toward you when it is sewn. There's a lot of bulk in that quilt and if it hits the wall behind the sewing machine, it can actually stop the quilt from feeding through as you sew! If this happens while you are sewing a decorative stitch, it will cause the stitch to become distorted.

Similarly, if the quilt falls off the table, weight of it will pull on the section you're trying to quilt, distorting the stitches and making the quilt harder to handle and keep straight. It could possibly pull enough to break a needle. It will certainly pull hard enough to distort any decorative stitches you are sewing.

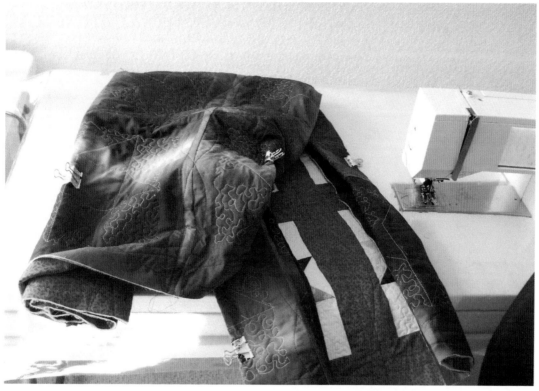

Here, I've used binder clips from an office supply store to hold the rolls of the quilt securely while I sew down the top row joining strips.

6. Quilted Borders

Adding a quilted border is a great way to spice up a quilt, and to make a small quilt just a little bit bigger.

Quilted borders are easy to add to any finished quilt that does not have the binding on it yet.

The borders can be as wide as you want to make them and require very little calculation.

The entire process of adding a quilted border is very similar to building and quilting your blocks. However, on the borders there are a few additional considerations and suggestions. You will need additional fabric for the border top and back, for the joining strips, and for a longer binding than you might have planned for. You'll also need additional batting.

The easiest border to add is a plain quilted border that frames the quilt. The borders will be trimmed to the size needed after they are quilted.

I would recommend that you do not use any complicated block designs in your borders because of the way the borders are attached. It is very possible to calculate out a complicated design, if you factor in the joining strips (which may overlap parts of the blocks if the blocks are constructed with ¼″ seam allowances) and the binding (because we recommend a wider than traditional binding). However, if you build your border blocks with these factors in mind, you could construct a very intricate border.

I highly recommend using the same fabric for your borders and your border top joining strips. If you use a contrasting color for the joining strips, understand the contrasting fabric will show in the corners, where the joining strips for the second set of borders overlap the first border.

Begin by measuring all four sides of your quilt. If your quilt measurements vary slightly from each other, you can use your border to bring them back to uniform length. Simply make the final cut to the border (when trimming, after quilting) the exact length you want the side of your quilt to be. Then slightly stretch or gather the quilt as it is joined to the border.

I suggest that you cut your top fabric at least 1½″ wider than your desired finished size and at least 2″ longer than what your quilt measures on each side for a small to medium sized quilt. For a larger quilt cut the top border fabric 4″ or more larger all the way around. Much of that will be taken up by quilting and trimming.

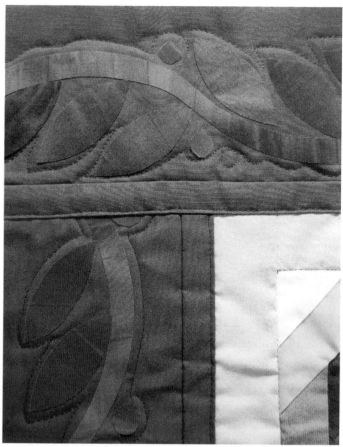

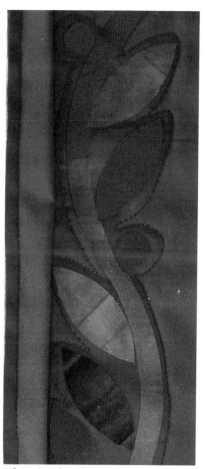

Better planning would have had the vines connect from border to border, around the corner.

The vine border before it was attached to the quilt.

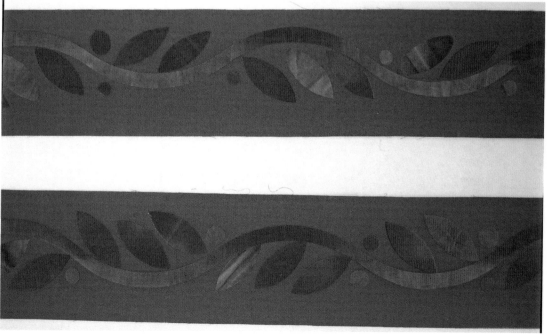

Two borders, before quilting or trimming.

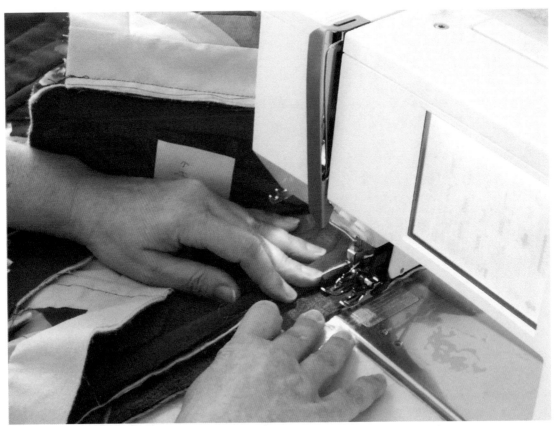

Adding a border is a quick and easy way to make a quilt larger.

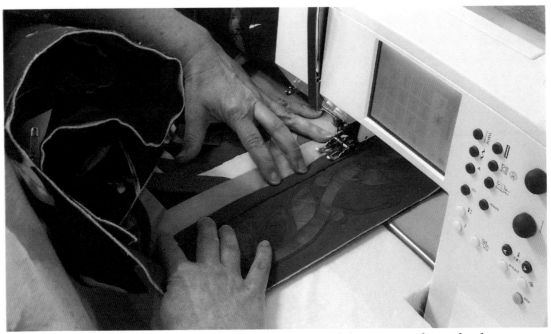

The sewing is easy because the bulk of the quilt is always on the left as you attach your borders.

Cut the first set of borders the same length (plus allowances) as the longer side of your quilt. To calculate the second set of borders, add twice the width of your desired finished border to the length of the shorter side of the quilt and cut your second set of borders (plus allowances) to that size.

For instance, if your quilt is 36″ x 45″ and you want to add 4″ borders, cut the first set of borders 5½″ x 47″ (it will be trimmed to 4″ x 45″). Cut the second set of borders 46″ x 5½″ (36″ + 4″ + 4″ = 44″ + 2″ allowance = 46″). This border will be trimmed to 4″ x 44″. The finished quilt will now be 44″ x 53″. Cut your joining strips the same length, exactly, as the **desired final border length**.

Layer, smooth, pin, and quilt your border panel, just as described in the Quilting chapter. Make sure your backing fabric and batting are at least 1″ larger all the way around.

When you have your borders quilted, measure them and mark the spot at which you'll trim them with a pin or a washable marker. Measure twice! You don't want to cut the borders too short.

Use the same techniques from the Trimming chapter; however it is a little more complicated with the longer border pieces. My best advice is to use as many rulers as you have. Start at the corner, making sure that the corner is square, then measure along the border, leaving the corner ruler in place. Make sure that the edges are straight and that the border is an even width.

Pin the joining strips to the border, starting at the ends, then pin the center. Finish pinning evenly along the border. Sew the borders on using a fat ¼″ seam, exactly the same way you joined the rows of your quilt.

Join the first set of borders to your quilt by sewing them on and quilting down the top joining strip. Join the second set of borders the same way, finishing by folding over and stitching down the top joining strip using a straight or decorative stitch.

For a border with a vine, as in the photos, be sure to leave at least 1½″ on all sides of the design for the trimming, joining, and binding allowance. You may also want to plan your corners better than I did. Next time, I will decorate the corners of the second set of borders after I have joining everything up. This will allow me to customize the vine curve, so it meets up with the vine on the first set of borders.

7. Binding

The **finishing** touch!

Like dressing up for a date and putting on that last pretty touch, the binding on your quilt says *"I'm done and ready to meet the world."*

I love the process of binding, of covering the raggedy quilt edges with gorgeously turned fabric that is beautifully stitched.

I love thinking about who the quilt is going to, and often I start dreaming of my next quilt as I sew the very last stitches on the binding.

My basic binding is wide, done all by machine, and features my "pretty corners" technique.

Give it a try for a beautifully *finished* quilt!

Binding, just like about everything else, is something I do my own way, and it's a way that really works for me. Please modify these steps or measurements to suit you. Read through the steps before you begin because I switch the order of things around from what you might be expecting.

I like my bindings wide, **cut on the lengthwise grain**, sewn to the back of the quilt first and finished on top with a straight or decorative stitch. I use my walking foot for sewing the binding onto the back.

Now, I should tell you that my daughter Sarah laughs out loud when she hears me talk about all the steps I take to put on a binding. Apparently, she can twitch her nose, and the binding just sews itself on perfectly, without measurement or care. Don't I wish I had that talent! But my point is this: I may overdo the measuring now because my first quilts had some horrifying bindings. I had no idea what I was doing and made many mistakes. If you have a binding method that already works for you, please feel free to use it and incorporate any of my tips that might help you.

As mentioned previously, while I calculate fabric purchase to match my quilt width, I always start my cutting with the binding, before cutting any joining strips.

A half a yard of fabric can bind a 60″ x 60″ quilt, but that's a lot of joining of short strips of fabric. I much prefer to cut what I need from a yard of fabric (setting aside the excess), which can produce about 540″ of binding, enough for a king-sized quilt.

Calculating Your Binding

Use the whole quilt measurement (the length of all four sides added together) and add an additional 20″ for seams and finishing. Divide that number by 36 to see how many 1 yard strips, roughly, are needed for your binding, rounding up to the next highest number.

For example, if I have a quilt of 12 blocks, and each block is 16″, my quilt will measure 48″ x 64″. 48+48+64+64 = 224. Add the extra 20″ for making connections (224 + 20 = 244). Divide 244 by 36″ (1 yard) 244/36 = 6.7. Round up to 7. This means I need 7 strips, each 1 yard long, to make my binding.

If I am using a piece of fabric for my binding that is 1½ yards long (54″) I cut 5 strips (244/54 = 4.5 rounds up to 5). If I am using fabric that is 2 yards long (72″), I cut 4 strips (244/72 = 3.4 rounds up to 4).

I prefer a 2½″ wide binding, but you can cut yours any width that you like.

Cut and Sew the Binding Strips

Once the binding strips are cut, you'll need to join them into one long strip. When joining binding strips, layer the ends with right sides together with a slight overlap, as shown below. It's much easier to sew the seam from corner to corner when the fabric is overlapped, rather than flush with one another. Sew the seam and finger press the seam open and trim the excess off with scissors.

I don't press the binding in half lengthwise, and I only starch the fabric if it has not been cut on the lengthwise grain.

Overlap strips and sew corner to corner.   *Finger press the seam open and trim to a ¼″ seam allowance.*

Measure and Sew the Binding On

Using the finished block size times the number of blocks, calculate what the length of each side of the quilt *should* be, not what it actually is. Measure the binding for each side before sewing it on.

You'll start by sewing down just one corner, leaving a long tail of binding behind it, removing the quilt from the sewing machine, and then measuring and pinning that side of the quilt binding only. Following are the steps.

Sew the Corner

Sew the binding to the back side of the quilt, raw edges together, with the binding lightly folded in half lengthwise but not pressed in half. Use a **fat ¼"seam,** just like when sewing on the joining strips.

Start by leaving 20" to 25" hanging, and start 8" to 12" from a corner. Going in a clockwise direction toward the corner, sew the binding onto the quilt, stopping a fat ¼" away from the edge, and back stitchi
ng.

Remove the quilt to make the corner fold as shown. First extend the binding 90° from the side you were sewing it to, then fold it over to lay flat along the upcoming edge.

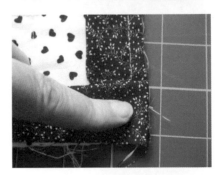

Pin the corner securely, making sure the fold is even with the edge of the quilt. Start stitching at the edge of the quilt, sewing just a couple of inches past that corner, on the new side.

Cut threads and take the quilt out of the sewing machine. Measure the binding for the next side of the quilt.

Measure

Measure the binding only, starting at the sewn corner and put a pin in the binding at the measurement where the next quilt corner *should* be. Line that pin up with the edge of your quilt and pin the binding to the quilt.

Pin the center of the quilt and binding together and continue to pin, evenly, until the binding is pinned to the quilt at every 4″ to 6″. If you have to stretch the quilt slightly to get it to match the binding, stretch it evenly over the whole side. Do the same if you need to take up a little extra quilt.

By measuring each side of the binding before sewing it on, you ensure that the finished quilt will be square.

Sew the binding on this side of the quilt and complete the corner. Cut threads after securing the next corner, and repeat the measuring, pinning, and sewing until you get to the last edge of your quilt.

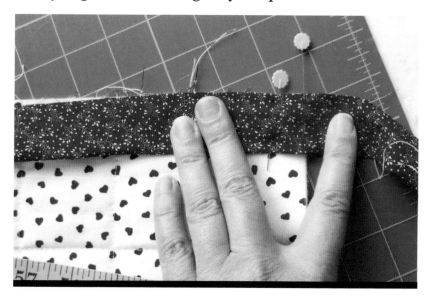

The pin on the right indicates where the corner should be. The pin on the left is where I've secured the binding to the quilt.

Join the Ends

The last edge is harder to measure and pin, but I usually give it a try by smoothing the loose binding ends flat onto the quilt and pinning up to about 16″ from where I started sewing. Sew to that pin, and then take the quilt out of the sewing machine and place this section on a flat surface.

You'll need a marking tool to mark the spot to join the two ends, using the same type of connection as when joining your strips to make your binding.

Smooth down both ends of the remaining binding strips, making sure that they are taut, but not too tight or too loose. Select a spot in the middle where the loose ends meet, and mark across the top edges of the binding.

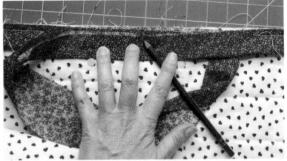

The two dots on the right sides of the fabric are going to be facing each other at their joining seam.

Align the two dots, facing each other, in the upper left-hand corner and pin. Here the marking pencil is pointing to the spot where the dots align.

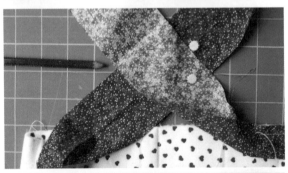

When you have them pinned, double check that the dots are still touching on the facing fabrics. Sew from the dots to the opposite intersection, exactly the same as joining binding strips.

120

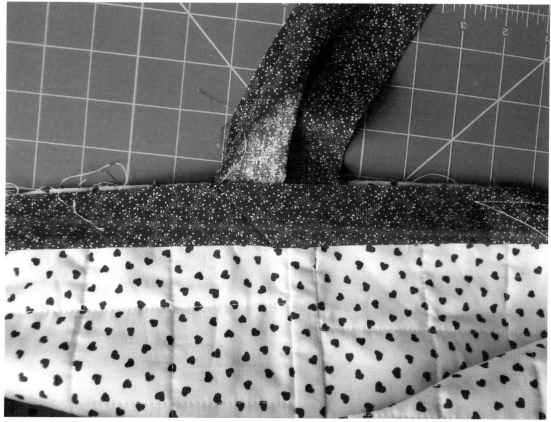

Before cutting the excess binding, make sure that it lays flat.

Before you trim the excess off the binding strips, give the binding a gentle fold and smooth it out over the quilt, making sure there is just the right amount of binding to finish the quilt. If the binding is too baggy or too tight, unsew the seam and repeat from the smoothing step on the previous page.

If the binding is just right, finger press the seam open and then trim the excess off the seam.

Pin the rest of the binding in place, and sew it to the quilt. Sew over your starting threads and back stitch to secure the thread ends.

Fold the binding over to the top of the quilt and machine sew it down, just like sewing down the top joining strip. Use a straight stitch or decorative stitch, regular thread or a decorative thread. Remember to change sewing machine feet if you are using a decorative stitch.

Pretty Corners

The binding corners on the top of the quilt can sometimes be confusing. I've developed a little technique that works every time to give me nice crisp corners and a binding that I am very happy with.

As you sew toward each corner, stop sewing about 6″ from the corner and pin the binding on the upcoming edge. That helps keep the binding in place as you turn the corner.

Next, using a strong pin (I like corsage pins), press the top fold of the binding in front of you down into itself, **off the edge of the quilt**. You'll be pushing the binding fabric off the edge of the batting and down onto your sewing machine bed. This puts tension on both sides of the binding—the side you are sewing and the upcoming side—and it helps create a lovely corner.

While holding this portion of the binding down with the pin, fold into place the binding on the edge that you are sewing and hold the fold. Slide the pin out of the corner, sticking the tip of it into the edge of the corner fold.

Folding the binding edges in this order creates a smooth corner on both sides of the quilt.

Push the pin all the way through the quilt and hold it there lightly.

Sewing slowly, hold the corner with the tip of the pin until the sewing machine needle is just a few stitches away from the pin. Take the pin out, and sew to just over the next side binding.

Put the sewing machine needle down and pivot the quilt, continuing on until done.

Here's a corner of the binding on the top of the quilt and below is a corner on the back of the quilt.

Congratulations,

you finished!

Dear Reader,

Thank you so much for buying my book and reading through it this far!

I have been teaching quilting for many years and something that I hear over and over—in person, via e-mail, and comments on my blog posts and my videos—is people saying, *"Thank you for saying it's okay to not be perfect!"* I say it all the time, and I'll keep on saying it. I don't strive to make perfect quilts. I make many, many quilts, and to me *done* is so much better than *perfect*.

If you enjoyed making a quilt using the techniques from this book, I'd love to hear from you. I love e-mail, and I love photos, if you'd like to share them. In fact, would you consider teaching someone else to quilt, using this book? You will find it very rewarding!

Lastly, I believe in giving more than expected whenever possible. For that reason, I often post updates, new quilt designs and videos, —all free—on my website and blog and my video channel. Please visit www.crazyshortcutquilts.com for more quilting goodies from me to you.

With my warmest regards,

Resources

The pattern shown on page 16 is by Debbie Caffrey, Debbie's Creative Moments, and is available from her on her website www.debbiescreativemoments.com.

The gorgeous bargello quilt on page 17 is used by permission from Ruth Blanchet and the pattern is available from her site, Arbee Designs, www.arbeedesigns.com.

The vines and leaves on the *Pineapple Log Cabin* quilt, pages 108 through 112 were created with Leaves Galore Templates designed by Sue Pelland. They are available from her at http://suepellanddesigns.com.

The quilt featured on page 21 was made by Sarah Raffuse and was originally featured in our book *Crazy Shortcut Quilts*. The book is available at many independently owned quilt shops and at Amazon.com in print and in e-book form. *Crazy Shortcut Quilts* teaches you how to make quilt-as-you-go quilts that look like crazy quilts,using fat quarters and the decorative stitches of the sewing machine to do all the quilting.

The quilts on pages 24, 77, and 80 are from *Quilt As You Go {reimagined}* by Marguerita McManus and Sarah Raffuse. The book is available in print from Amazon.com and in e-book format for the Kindle, Kobo and Nook.

Many of the projects hanging on the design wall on page 33 and the quilt top on page 14, were made by friends or by sellers on ebay.com.

If you would like to see Marguerita's sewing and quilting tips, please visit her YouTube channel at **http://www.youtube.com/CrazyShortcutQuilts**. You will often see a quilt she is working on in the background of the video.

Marguerita blogs and shares her quilting ideas on the website she created for her first book at www.crazyshortcutquilts.com.

You will see many references to comfort in this book and you can find out more by reading *Sew & Quilt in Comfort* by Marguerita McManus. The book is available in print and for the Kindle through Amazon.com.

Please contact Marguerita at MMQuilts@gmail.com.

Quilt As You Go {reimagined}

Quilt As You Go with a modern, fresh twist! No one will ever never know your quilts are quilt-as-you-go and that's the twist.

This book teaches a few modern twists on a very popular technique which results in simple, easy to make quilts that can be made from "fat quarters", "jelly rolls" and "charms" as well as yardage and scraps.

Just like with *Crazy Shortcut Quilts* and *Finish (almost) Any Quilt*, the basics are here but the techniques are adaptable to your tastes and ideas.

New Techniques For A Modern Look

We devised new techniques both for making quilts and for hiding the joining strips—you won't be able to tell that it's quilt-as-you-go. Modern design and fresh fabrics were our inspiration and simple, easy quilts are the result. Made from Fat Quarters, Jelly Rolls, Charms and scraps, these quilts are just the starting point for your new quilt-as-you-go direction.

What's different from our other quilt-as-you-go books?

The quilts are made of pieced blocks and the joining process is changed slightly for each of the four quilts in the book. We are using straight stitches to quilt with instead of decorative stitches, but of course you can use either.

This book is small—only 78 pages—with just four quilt patterns, but enough changes to spark your imagination for making many quilts.

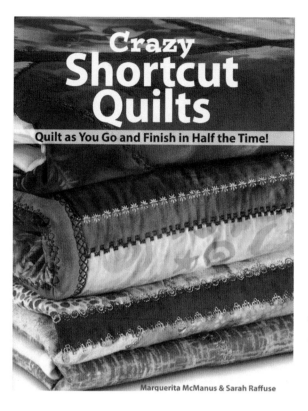

Crazy Shortcut Quilts teaches you how to make crazy quilts using fat quarters and fast cutting. You use the decorative stitches of your sewing machine to quilt-as-you-go.

Many of the techniques from *Crazy Shortcut Quilts* are incorporated in this book, *Finish (Almost) Any Quilt*; however, the crazy cutting and planning your own quilt are unique to *Crazy Shortcut Quilts*.

Available at quilt shops, bookstores, and Amazon.com.

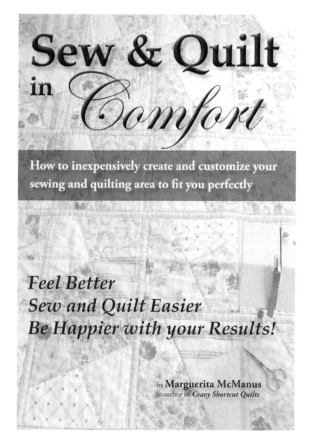

Sew & Quilt in Comfort is about the ergonomics of sewing comfortably and how to inexpensively create a custom, flat, sewing surface that fits your sewing machine and you perfectly.

Using ordinary materials and no power tools, you can create a flat surface that will make machine quilting easier instantly.

Available in print from Amazon.com and for the Kindle, Kobo and Nook.

About the Author

Marguerita McManus is the co-author of *Crazy Shortcut Quilts* and *Quilt As You Go {reimagined}*. She is the author and publisher of *Finish (almost) Any Quilt* and *Sew & Quilt in Comfort*.

She has been quilting and teaching quilting since the latter portion of the 1990's and publishing since 2010.

Her philosophy of "done is better than perfect" helps her finish many quilts, none of which are prize winners but all of which are cherished.

She and her daughter, Sarah, make many quilts for charity and they both love trying new ideas in quilting.

Marguerita is the happy grandmother to Audrey and Violet Raffuse, and she spends her time learning, writing, quilting, traveling and making videos. She'd love to hear from you! Please contact her at **MMQuilts@gmail.com**.

36832758R00073

Made in the USA
Lexington, KY
06 November 2014